Peter

Your First Edition of
the truth

Gerry O'Halloran

edsy!!

If Only Politicians Had Brains

By

Terence P. O'Halloran

Design: Life Publications Limited

First published Copyright © 2001 Life Publications Limited,
88 Newland LINCOLN LN1 1YA
Internet Site: www.lifepublications.co.uk
E-mail: tpo@lifepublications.co.uk

Printed and bound in Great Britain by Hackman Print Group, Cambrian Ind. Park, Clydach Vale, Tonypandy, Rhondda, CF40 2XX.

A catalogue record for this book is available from the British Library.

Front cover artwork TIM MILNER, Cambridge.

ISBN 0-9506314-3-4 Hard Bound
ISBN 0-9506314-4 -2 Paperback

Dedicated to: Eleanor Downie and

my long-suffering staff.

Contents

Foreword

Few of us would start from here if we had the choice. The starting point for any project is seldom popular but it is where you are and you have no choice. That is how it was in 1971; having just joined the Financial Services industry from a career in engineering it seemed that I could know little, compared to others.

Organisations like the Consumers' Association particularly and, of course, Government Departments responsible for far-reaching legislation surely had access to the educational qualifications and experience to draw upon that made their pronouncements correct?

Yet something seemed strangely uncomfortable with what I was reading and what I knew from my studies and my then two years experience.

By 1974 I had written my first book with a view to informing the uninformed about a specific topic, Life Assurance. Those who had a public stage were misdirecting the cast.

Life is a theatre; and most people perform to their script each day, either by habit or in line with some defined discipline, like going to school or work.

So it is that I have used the theatre or rather televised theatre by way of an analogy to take you through technical issues in a light-hearted and hopefully instructive way. We are what we experience and our opinions and, therefore, our thoughts and our deeds come from that very essence of our lives models. Whether the life model centres on Dan Dare or the Goons or Jonathan Creek; love them or hate them, they create an impression.

It is perhaps difficult to be overly objective in a society where mainstream public television is unfit for children to watch after nine o'clock. Our basic language has been reduced to the 'f' word and sexually explicit innuendo. The media dictates its producers' 'norms', whilst pressurising officialdom to react to sensationalism. In short propagandist manipulation of the system is the order of the day.

Politicians no longer write their own speeches and do not, therefore, open their own hearts and minds for examination to those who are seeking representation at the highest level. Representation carries a responsibility with it, but is that responsibility upheld?

What of those who wish to sell their own books, magazines and association memberships as they masquerade as charities and public service organisations, which clearly they have long ceased to be?

The Treasury, the Department of Trade, the Consumers' Association, Financial Services Authority and many others have effectively been 'mystery shopped'.

By placing myself in a position where I would be taken through 'the processes' and having experienced them, I can now speak upon them first-hand. Authority and facts are now set to counter regulation and hypothesis. It appears to be extremely easy, as you will find, to confuse one with the other.

This, I am convinced, would have been the foreword to the book had you written it. It is probably worth reading the book just to see how much of your opinion is reflected in mine.

Experience tells me that the majority of people are dissatisfied with Government at all levels. They are also dissatisfied with those who drain the finite resources of public expenditure to provide themselves with a comfortable retirement and a position where they have absolutely no responsibility for their actions during their working lifetime.

If accountability and responsibility are to be the lot of the private sector, then surely it is only right and proper that accountability and responsibility have to be exercised in the public service?

They are not: and that has to change.

f Only Politicians Had Brains is not a book of theory.

It is a book of facts borne out of experience and research. It is far from dull and dreary.

I hope very much that you enjoy reading it, even though, at times, you may get a little tetchy with some of the things that you discover go on in our society in the name of democracy. Get angry if you must, but remember, it solves nothing. Getting even, now that is a different proposition.

10 March 2001

Preface

Terence O'Halloran is a qualified aircraft engineer who thirty years ago moved into financial services. He holds a Bachelor of Science degree in business administration and the equivalent of a Masters degree in insurance. He is a qualified financial planner.

Terence is a **very practical individual** who has devoted much of his time to organisations such as **British Junior Chamber** where he spent thirteen years working in the community in Gainsborough, Lincolnshire.

He has been on a number of national advisory committees and functional committees of the **Federation of Small Businesses** and was a founder member of that organisation over twenty-five years ago.

He is currently **President of the Lincoln Area** of the Lincolnshire Chamber of Commerce and Industry, a position that he feels helps the community as a whole.

Although television is mentioned quite a lot in the text, the author of this book is not particularly a television viewer. He quite simply does not have time. The lighter side of life appeals to **his sense of fun.**

Terence is no stranger to producing books, both as a publisher and also as an author. Most of his previous writings have been of a technical nature.

The thirty years of dealing with Government Departments at different levels and three 'mystery shopping' exercises have cost him money, but proved the point. They have created thousands of pages of evidence and a damning **story of ineptitude, conspiracy, extortion and waste.**

The author of '*If Only Politicians Had Brains*' walks his talk. **He lectures widely**, having lectured to workers on picket lines (in the nicest possible way; using a 'flip chart'). Terence has **'bricked up' a Civic Authority** and challenged those in the highest authority to explain their actions.

The one great thing about this book is its **authority and incisive truth**. It is a 'pick and dip' that will keep you on the edge of your seat and may even end up with you **banging on your politician's door.**

The parallels of what pass for 'entertainment' and 'real life' are actually drawn to illustrate that '*Yes, Prime Minister*' may not have been quite so wide of the 'real world' mark as may have been thought by many of the programme's viewers.

Thought process

An intelligent person's learning process may pass through three stages:

First, they learn the right answers.

Second, they learn the right questions.

Hopefully at the third stage, they may learn with experience, which questions are worth asking to get worthwhile answers.

CHAPTER 1

WOODEN HEADED POLITICS: A DESTRUCTIVE FORCE.

Every day we see more evidence of the fact that **politicians consider the general population** to be just **a mass of morons** who really do not know what is best for them.

Over the last twenty years **arrogance beyond the realms of acceptability** has reflected in the changes in society that are inevitable and yet accelerated in their implementation by politicians doing "what is good for us"; through a media which prescribes our fate and professional lobbyists who are paid protagonists for "the cause" (not the pop group).

Gone, it seems, are the genuine concerns of the person at number 22. They are **lost in the turmoil of mass-hysteria** generated by those who know 'so much more' **from the standpoint of almost complete ignorance**.

SMOKESCREENS

That is what the book is all about. It is about Government **diverting your attention** from what really matters to **what seems to matter**.

The local politics of **traffic calming** and **environmental improvement** decisions appear to be made on perceptions with **no accountable results** rather than structured and meaningful experimentation. Control freaks do things, seemingly, just to prove that they can.

Those stories are here for a purpose because they, too, form part of the **patchwork of delusion** that things are happening for a purpose, when in actual fact it is merely a **diversionary tactic** to take the inquisitive eye **away from a major issue**.

At a national level, the smokescreens become more sophisticated and **imbued with emotional attributes.**

Fox hunting, pensions mis-selling, endowment mortgages, BSE are all ploys to distract. How do fewer than one hundred people with CJD take centre stage when equally disturbing and indeed horrendously debilitating conditions like multiple sclerosis, Alzheimer's and leukaemia, which involve **tens of thousands of people** per disease or condition, get **pushed into the background?**

Cerebral palsy is something that people live with for twenty and thirty years and much needs to be done to eradicate it, and yet millions of pounds, if not **billions of pounds,** has been expended on **cultivating** what is now an international **political smokescreen** for other issues.

Whenever a major political issue comes up, suddenly they find a cow in the middle of Germany that has got BSE, or maybe it is Spain, but it is one of millions of cows, and it is front page. Doesn't that alarm you?

Haven't you wondered why **endowments** are getting such **bad press** whilst the one that you have that has just matured has produced **such exceptional results?**

Doesn't it seem odd that the people who are telling you in 'plain English' that the product that produces **three times more than it promises,** are the same people stating that endowments are something to be **feared and avoided**?

A smokescreen. A diversionary tactic to **discredit With-Profit Funds** to push people **towards** more **speculative** but Government **sponsored savings media** such as Individual Savings Accounts (ISAs). The statistics might not stack up, but **who worries about statistics?** The majority of citizens find statistics boring and an intrusion in the decision making process.

But where do they get their illusions from?

2

Politicians tell us that we have to ensure that BSE is driven out of the system by use of **a zero tolerance option**. There have been fewer than one hundred sufferers of CJD, which has still **no conclusive scientific link** with the aforementioned 'mad cow disease', BSE.

The mass murder of three million cattle was the politicians answer.

ANIMAL RIGHTS OR POLITICAL LOBBYISTS

Where were the animal rights activists whilst this slaughter was being perpetrated? Are they all vegetarian, perhaps, and felt justified in staying away? Was the RSPCA on its annual holiday or were the animals concerned too large? Why else would they have allowed such a travesty when they so ably **defend the fox?**

Where was the 'vegan' bank employee, Dawn Preston, the chairman of the Hunt Saboteurs Association?

It is like a massive game of Trivial Pursuit except that the stakes are high, the destruction permanent, the misery palpable and the individual cost excruciatingly real. More political energy has been expended on marginal, almost trivial matters, than on major issues.

The 'PARK BENCH' syndrome lives on.

The park bench syndrome? It is easy to discuss a park bench at length because its cost and facility is easily understood by the majority of councillors or politicians. Hours are expended on 'monuments', dubious works of 'art' and similar 'park bench' frippery. A new major initiative that costs millions and serves thousands, but is more difficult to get into the detail, is 'in and out' in a comparative trice.

We are now beset with **highly-paid professional complainers** who influence our lives to the extent that **we are afraid to cuddle our children** and more importantly, never ever embrace, comfort, pat, reward or have any other contact with anyone else's children **for fear** that we are accused of **molesting them**.

3

We must also be guarded in our approach to other human beings, for fear of sexual harassment or just plain interference in their 'private' affairs.

Was it a lack of police 'on the beat' that left a ten-year-old coloured boy to bleed to death in a London suburb? The problems highlighted by Damilola Taylor are far greater than those in authority will admit to. The problem is **fear of authoritarian retribution**. Racism is a multifaceted myth created in the minds of people who would otherwise never give it a second thought. **It generates political capital**.

THE FLAVOUR OF THE MONTH

And **where are our wooden chopping boards?**

Well they are **coming back into fashion**. Having been instructed to "remove and destroy ALL wooden chopping boards" and been the recipients of heavy fines and acrimonious debate, butchers can now proceed as they have instinctively known they should for centuries.

Back in days of yore the cabbage, bread, and meat all got the chop on the same wooden board. That was in the days when **80%-90% of everybody's earnings put food on the table and clothes on your back**. It was also a time of shepherd's pie and the use of 'left overs'. Remember soups and casseroles? We knew what went in and delighted at what came out.

These days when little more than 20% of earnings are spent on staple items such as food and clothes, the rasher of bacon left over from a Sunday treat of over a week ago will probably walk out of the fridge, tapping the side of the tin can holding the half-portion of beans that we thought we would save to go with it.

4

THE ACADEMIC ANSWER

The logic of authority says that we must **educate people** in the art of self-preservation by sticking more labels on more packaging that more illiterate and innumerate people can ignore or misunderstand. Once again 'they' are **treating the symptom rather than the cause,** following some manifestly 'intelligent' individual's theory that goes against everything that human nature has taught us over the last 6,000 years.

Our society's **prescription for the eradication of Aids** is to provide our youngsters with sex education: promoting **"Safe Sex"** with a mechanism that is inefficient. When it is used by youngsters with sharp finger-nails, a healthy appetite and a lack of attention to detail, then efficiency slips and reports of between 60% and 80% from the Family Planning Service would probably be generous. However, at least **their observations are based upon facts**.

One would think that the politicians would similarly have some regard for the 'failure factor' before declaring sex "safe" in advising the population concerning the eradication of **Aids**. Aids is **a killer disease**.

Surely **NO SEX would be a better message**. Religious teaching would support that rationale. Could <u>that</u> be a reason for ignoring the obvious do you think? Abstinence is a strength rather than a weakness, surely?

Even the commercial radio stations ask "Are you thinking about sex?" during the evening meal. Is there no escape?

Contrast **AIDS** then with **Mad Cow Disease**.

A REACTIONARY FORCE

BSE or *Bovine Spongiform Encephalopathy*, is not a new disease among cattle. It was highlighted in the early 1980s as a problem became more evident.

5

Now the one thing that we British are is **honest**. We love to share our misery. Let's **tell somebody** about the problem. You have seen them on *'Dinner ladies'*. "You tell me yours and I'll tell you mine" – with a little embellishment.

As has been stated: at the time that the Government decided to **slaughter three million cattle** there had been less than ten deaths from CJD <u>ever</u>.

There is **still no scientific proof** that there is a link between BSE and CJD: just as there is no proof that there is a link between Scrapie, the sheep equivalent and BSE, nor a similar disease that attacks cats and so on. There is a **lot of perception** and supposition that a link exists. The evidence was circumstantial yet the Government's reaction was **zero tolerance**.

Surely the **correct procedure** was to isolate, research, quantify and then take appropriate action to resolve the issues.

You may remember that Edwina Currie reacted in much the same way when "their Lordships" **contracted salmonella from some egg mayonnaise**, she had 80 million chickens slaughtered. (No more Currie's eggs for me.) With profound apologies to *Major Dennis Bloodknock.*

The source of the BSE 'scare' was much the same. An 'inconsequential' comment in the House of Commons by Stephen Dorrell MP was seemingly picked up by *a tabloid paper*, perhaps it would **help to reflect** on which one, and the next thing there were headlines screaming:

"Stop eating beef."

Compare the tragedy of Aids and the huge numbers involved and the Government's reaction to that. Spend millions of pounds of taxpayers' money on research and special facilities in hospitals desperately short of resources for mainstream medical and surgical conditions, whilst concurrently promoting 'safe sex' and slaughtering cattle.

The responses are somewhat inconsistent.

6

THE REAL STORY – THE FACTS

The story was made even more ludicrous when *Rotary International* in 1998 started a campaign to donate cattle to Uganda. A lot of the Ugandan herds had died off through drought.

Would it not have been better to have **sent the cattle we did not want** (strictly monitored of course) to Uganda to **feed people who were dying of starvation** in their thousands; than to now, five years on, still be trying to dispose of the carcasses of those wretched beasts that have, since their slaughter, been taking up valuable space in improvised freezer houses pending their total destruction?

Millions of tons of meat that **has yet to be proved to be marginally injurious to human health** has cost billions of pounds to remove from circulation.

Only the Trident missile scheme has cost more in the history of our country.

How many real problems could have used those billions of wasted pounds effectively? Who caused the problem initially?

In 1974 the Arab world decided that OPEC countries would raise the price of oil.

As a means of conserving oil the EU produced a directive confirming that farmers rearing cattle could **reduce the cooking temperature** for 'high protein' feeds that contained animal offal, from 400° C to 270° C.

Many farmers were unaware of the non-vegetarian nature of the feed because the sacks were not marked properly with a list of ingredients.

BSE manifested itself some years later. You will find a whole host of **coincidences** of similar magnitude.

Did the bureaucrats who may have got it wrong investigate the circumstances? Nothing has appeared in any of the official reports, not even the most recent **sixteen million pound [STERLING] masterpiece**.

Has the producer of the feed been 'brought to book'?

The one aspect of Government and its officials that stands out, is their **arrogance in adversity** coupled with their unerring ability to point the finger; so that someone else pays.

Clinical tests on rats with BSE are said to prove a trans-mutation of the virus but, with the extremely high doses of contaminated tissue being fed to the rats, they probably developed 'piles' as well.

The **compliant** in our society are **the victims**.

The farmers could have **taken their livestock** and despatched it to the offices of the newspapers or perhaps the studios at **News At Ten**, as it was then, and has now become again, and **let the whole lot loose.**

Perhaps then **intelligence** would override **arrogance**.

They might even have dropped them off in the middle of the M1 motorway with the entreaty:

"If you think you can look after them better than we can, now is your chance to try."

"And **if you want to slaughter them, you take 'em.**"

But farmers are **law-abiding citizens** and complied with having their livelihood taken from them meekly.

Ministry of Agriculture, Fisheries and Food
Rm B28C Government Bldgs, Hook Rise South, Tolworth, Surrey, KT6 7NF
Telephone: 0181 330 4411 ext 8220   GTN: 3836 8220
Direct line: 0181 330 8220   FAX: 0181 330 8644
E-mail:

Your reference:
Our reference: BOV 427

14 April 1998

Dear Mr O'Halloran

BOVINE SPONGIFORM ENCEPHALOPATHY (BSE)

Thank you for your letter of 3 March to the Minister about BSE. I have been asked to reply and apologise for the delay in doing so.

The scientific evidence linking BSE and nvCJD has been considerably strengthened since SEAC made its original statement in March 1996. Two studies, one by Dr Bruce in Scotland and one by Professor Collinge in London, who is a member of SEAC, have both shown that the agent from the brains of nvCJD cases behaves in experimental conditions in the same way as the BSE agent. In Dr Bruce's case the BSE agent behaved the same way whether from cattle or from experimental sheep or from cases of FSE in cats and the finding that the agent from the brains of patients with nvCJD behaves in the same way has led SEAC to the conclusion that the agents causing the two diseases are the same. That is a very powerful conclusion and I do not believe that scientists working in this area would dispute this.

Yours sincerely

T Mitchell
BSE Correspondence Section

9

CHAPTER 2

A NEW BREED OF EXPERT – THE UNINFORMED

Tommy Cooper always struck me as being the epitome of the truly great magician. Just like Les Dawson playing the piano out of key, the trick has to go wrong precisely at the right time to create the laugh, the joke, and the music has to be intelligible yet so grossly wrong as to be comical, for everything to succeed.

The Paddington, Ladbroke Grove and Hatfield rail disasters all fall into exactly the same category: timing, and juxtapositioning.

There is nothing funny about people losing their lives. Yet the huge amount of money that has been spent on analysis of those 'tragedies' is so out of proportion to the scale of the problem.

THE POWER OF THE MEDIA

The journalistic licence and headline speculation that epitomise the British media overplay the cards to such an extent that one wonders if a train could ever run safely again. The British rail network is one of the safest rail networks in the world and arguably one of the more efficient.

Of course the "bring back British Rail" lobby would not agree with that, but then they have a point to prove, and like Tommy Cooper, are experts at getting the timing right to make sure that the trick does not succeed, but the 'entertainment' or message does.

The pictures of the Hatfield disaster **actually exemplify the safety** of our high-speed trains in an emergency situation. Four people died in what was described in the newspapers as a "scene of horror".

Fifty-five people have died on the roads in a sparsely populated county in a six-month period. Where are the national headlines? Road accidents **are "normal accidents"**. Tell that to the relatives.

A SENSE OF PROPORTION

Thousands have died across the nation and yet **where is the allotment** of **£15 billion** by the transport minister to **make our roads safer**? To ease congestion, to provide bypasses, instead of sleeping policemen and chicanes that exacerbate rather than alleviate the problems, we should have comprehensive road network improvements.

Of course there is **more traffic on the M25**; that is what it was designed for. The local roads have proportionately less traffic. **The plan worked**. Read the statistics.

Would the expenditure cut down the number of people killed on the roads? International statistics seem to indicate that it probably would.

And if it was by a mere 10% it would still save ten times more lives, and a greater multiplier more of serious injury, than the extra 'rail cash' will save in the wake of the **'media' designated 'carnage'** that is reported on our railways.

In time statistics may well prove that the disruption of the railways; 'established' timetables in the aftermath of 'Hatfield' has already cost **more lives in road accidents** than would have been the case if a more pragmatic approach had been adopted.

Seemingly a young man at the controls of a diesel train was at fault for the Paddington disaster. He inadvertently went through a red light.

RESPONSIBLE ACCEPTANCE

The Ladbroke Grove disaster was publicly laid at the feet of a driver whose attention was diverted whilst driving a lethal vehicle at high speed with

12

hundreds of passengers in his charge. If a young man 'went through' a traffic light during his journey in a motor vehicle 'all hell' would fall on him. There is **an inconsistency that is unacceptable.**

Yet from the press and, one has to say, from the reported trade union responses, "one cannot hold an individual responsible," we have **to find a scapegoat** somewhere else. The lights were poorly placed. How many road traffic lights are poorly placed?

Like Les Dawson, if you play the note out of tune and try and take the emphasis off what would perhaps be a serious piece of music; you turn it into **a farce**.

In either of those two circumstances, in the former where two passenger trains collided at peak travelling times, and in the latter where a high-speed passenger train struck a goods train crossing the main line, **the level of injury was substantially less than one might have expected in the circumstances**. Yet where is the glowing report on passenger safety? It is well hidden behind the sensational headlines and speculation. Few facts: just speculation that clouds the issues. But, it **makes good television.**

If these had been motor vehicles; say **a luxury coach** similar to the one in America where **23 British tourists died** because a tyre 'blew out', the so-called "carnage" would have been quite evident.

The tourist bus that left the road in South Africa provided a very real example of what percentage of the travelling public in one vehicle can expect to be maimed, injured, or even killed in a road traffic accident; a far higher percentage one has to say than any of the major rail accidents, reports of which are undermining the public confidence. **Gross misrepresentation and expediency** exhibited by parliamentarians, and of course, sensationalist, self-seeking lobbyists.

Just like Cooper (not Henry, he was a boxer) and Dawson, one has to be very clever to appear a fool. Given that perhaps the public can see through the charade in the media and the reaction within the Houses of Parliament, those trying to cloud the rail safety issue may well be **fools attempting to appear clever.**

One could argue that the huge amount of publicity; and the expenditure of billions of pounds that is being concentrated on a 'few weeks' replacement of, reportedly, hundreds of miles of track, will be beneficial.

The implementation over the next eight years of warning bells and buzzers will give the public confidence, and allow those who actually rely on the trains to get to and from their place of work, or leisure, an **overriding sense of understanding** when they arrive four hours late.

EXPERIENCE TO DO THE JOB?

One could perhaps ask the question; **who is the rail regulator**? What is his qualification, and just how good would he be if he had to run a railway? But then that is asking for an answer to a question that is, of course, unanswerable. Would it be **more prudent to employ the expert regulator to run Railtrack** as his salary is a fraction of the erstwhile or incumbent CEO?

It is an irony that the misinformation seems irrefutably designed to undermine commercial practice, and to provide large fees and percentages of 'compensation packages' that the courts dish out, from what they see as 'social funds', to the lawyers conducting the case.

In this case the 'conductor' (regulator) does not play a note that would be in any way comparable to those produced by Les Dawson to achieve the resultant accolade for having provided a good performance. But **it does make good theatre**; containing something for the journalists to write up and the politicians to respond to. The opportunities for television are immense. Voyeurism has never had it so good.

As Tommy Cooper would have said "it's not like that, it's like that." One has to be very careful in **quoting national newspapers** in particular, but also the media in general, on any given topic.

14

A MATTER OF TRUST

In a recent survey of over 1000 people, **only 2%** (that is 20 out of the 1000 questioned) felt that the written or verbal 'utterings' of the media **were trustworthy**. That is a sad indictment on a major accepted form of mass communication. It seems that we only **read newspapers** and watch television news **for their entertainment** value. But the media does hold sway with all levels of authority.

Radio news is seen as more trustworthy, presumably because it is more pithy and therefore more factually based. However, one has to go with the flow on occasions and take general principles at their face value.

Take the case of the two boys who so **callously murdered the Bulgar toddler**. From what one reads and from reports at the time of the trial, the two boys set out to do damage to another human being purely for their own entertainment and self-gratification. **They will be freed; and hunting will be banned.**

Myra Hindley probably falls into the same category of analysis, and yet 'human rights' being what 'human rights' are, these people will probably **be released back into the community** and may well damage a member of society again. There is an equal argument to say that they may not, but, they will be able to do what they, personally, feel is right.

In comparison to erring on the side that "these individuals will not damage society", and remembering **the horrendous way** in which they did **offend in the first place**, the loss of ability for some individuals to continue their chosen occupation because they 'offended' some regulator or lobbyist somewhere by not dotting an 'i' or crossing a 't' is a travesty.

THE ABILITY TO PAY – ACQUIESCENCE

Many **self-employed and small business proprietors** have been subject to financially **damaging fines**, which either drove them out of business or led to their being 'struck off' a register that enabled them to work.

It could be because the business person's **'capital adequacy'** was less than prescribed. A politician can borrow beyond his capital and run the country whilst presiding over the termination of a citizen's ability to earn a living for being **less than £10,000** solvent.

The situation might reflect the circumstances of the **nursing home proprietor who had his business closed down** because of a completely fallacious and inccurate BBC exposé. He was just unlucky to get 'chosen' for the programme. A bank seemingly wishing to ingratiate itself with one 'customer' at the expense of another created a similar travesty.

Murderers (terrorists being murderers who commit murder for political reasons rather than personal ones) are **being released** from the Maze prison. Society, you, will have paid compensation to them for having been incarcerated in the first place. **Many are self-confessed assassins.**

Compare the Bulgar assailants who were put into detention at Her Majesty's pleasure following a trial in which **they were innocent until proven guilty**. The ex-doctor **Shipman** cannot now stand trial for "over 200 suspected murders" because he **"will not receive a fair trial"**.

A QUESTION OF INNOCENCE

Many of those from the **business fraternity** who lose their right to work are undoubtedly **guilty until proven innocent**.   That seems to be the commercial risk that they took when they went into business.

The fact that they **serve society unstintingly** for long hours and low reward seems to be lost on that 'society'. A recent Federation of Small Businesses survey put 37% of such entrepreneurs in pure survival mode, working to survive, at subsistence levels, **without Government help**.

The new millennium was heralded by a newspaper report of **a 'madam'** who had run a brothel and made multi-million pounds of personal wealth from the process, being **fined £6,000**.

But a £6,000 fine is **only two-thirds** of what a **financial adviser** would have **to pay for failing to keep some paperwork in a prescribed fashion.** One has to say that the earnings of the two comparable "businesses" could not be further apart on the relevant scales.

The 'madam' was innocent until proven guilty. The financial advisor was guilty until proven innocent; with no mechanism that could be relied upon to prove that innocence.

For a regulator the rules are the rules and you either keep them or break them. There are no halfway houses. Human rights have not and seemingly do not apply to such groups. Perhaps if they read this they will regulate prostitution – it could be more profitable than the criminal courts!

Frank, the **farmer, had some wayward slurry**, the equivalent of sewage, which seeped into a waterway leading to a visit by the environmental health authorities. The tribunal that he attended found him guilty, but the fine was not decided until they had **vetted his accounts to determine how much** they thought he could afford, without, of course, driving him into immediate bankruptcy.

The tens of thousands of pounds that the farmer paid fails to compare with the exit from court of a driver whose attention, seemingly, was temporarily distracted from the road (for over half a mile). The subsequent accident, for which he was **found guilty of manslaughter,** resulted in the death of three people. **He went free with a small fine**.

BIG IS BEAUTIFUL

The final ignominy is when the smaller business proprietor suffers a regulatory impasse because of the actions of a national or international organisation acting out of financial expediency.

Helen ran a very successful business in the North East of England and created an **estimated value within her firm of around £400,000** over a seven-year period. Ten of her customers (she had two and a half thousand) fell into a category which became the subject of a national dispute.

A major corporation, which also had a number of customers in this particular category, was being sued for compensation and assessed that it would be cheaper to pay the compensation than go through a very expensive court procedure to prove the claims invalid or quantify the compensation to a low level.

Their decision set the precedent for the market place, and ten times the £30,000 that **they decided as an arbitrary, non-calculated, figure for compensation put Helen out of business**. Not only did Helen suffer, but also two and a half thousand customers suddenly lost their representation and their ability to conduct business in a way that was comfortable for them.

Was the compensation due? Ironically; probably not. Once the calculations had been done, a sum that would have been affordable to Helen and allowed her to maintain her business would have been payable.

However, politicians and those who make the rules have little regard to market consequences in such circumstances. Expediency, getting the job done, **ticking a box** and breathing a sigh of relief, is all that seems to concern them.

Their salary and indexed pension (non-contributory of course), is safe for another day.

CHAPTER 3

THE MEDIA'S RESPONSIBILITY

Is it the media that creates so much of our moral, and thereby environmental, hazard with the way that it reports incidents or portrays life?

Looking at the statistics today there are **no more indecent assaults, murders, rapes or pillages than there have ever been**. It is a part of life that a minute percentage of the total population are 'bad' men and women who do dastardly things. But the media build things up out of all proportion.

PARENTAL PARANOIA

Is it **any wonder that parents are paranoid about allowing their children to walk or cycle to school**, or to walk down the country lane that leads to the bus stop? To allow them to go on a public bus or train on their own seems a grave manifestation of parental callousness in the face of danger.

The media amplifies the very behaviour that responsible parents would wish their offspring to avoid.

TV affects impressionable teenagers. Equally their parents and grandparents are treated to the same **constant diet of the very worst of our society**. Some of the offerings are 'hilariously' funny; '*Men Behaving Badly*' teaches our young men the art of confident conversation and humorous repartee.

Of course it depicts life. So does going to the toilet but it is not acceptable to the majority of decent people requiring entertainment. However, the ratings are a barometer of popularity.

Ironically **Her Majesty the Queen was reported as having 'poor' viewing figures at 9.9 million viewers** on the same day as the highest audience for any other production for the whole day was 9.8 million. The 'day' was Christmas Day 2000.

Have all **teenage children** under the age of eighteen to be in bed by 9 o'clock? If this form of 'acceptable' entertainment is reflecting real life, which it is not in most people's experience, then **surely eleven o'clock** should be the 'watershed' in these days when many parents allow their children to stay up later, thus reflecting 'real life'.

What is it that the presenter of *'Crimewatch'* says at the end of the programme?

"Please don't have nightmares. What the programme is depicting is only a very small portion of society and an **extremely rare** occurrence."

A responsible journalistic statement that is overshadowed by its contemporary's insensitive oversights.

FACT OR FICTION

It is just **when it affects you** that it becomes a **major incident**.

It suits news editors to have us on the edge of our seats. Is that why we buy newspapers: to see what the next disaster, the latest conflict, the juiciest piece of gossip is? That is the form of writing that journalists use.

Sensationalist, explosive, and, for the most part, fatuous. Much of the rhetoric is worthy of some of the best novel writers, but at least in the latter case, people know and appreciate that **it is fiction**.

You might retort, "Well, people know that the 'soaps' are fiction."

Why then do people send birthday cards, sympathy cards and wreaths at the appropriate moments following a particular episode in one or other of the major 'soaps'?

Why is it that the Prime Minister of the United Kingdom asked a question in the House of Commons about a fictitious character named Deirdre who was incarcerated in a make-believe jail, in a make-believe story, on a very real television set thus creating a national uproar?

What sort of society have we got ourselves into? What sort of agenda does the Prime Minister have? Robin Cook took time to acknowledge the "great contribution to the nation's security that James Bond had made". He's a fictional character.

No, not Robin Cook, James Bond.

Radio drama and book drama may well associate with fiction because they rely on the imagination of the listener or the reader to interpret what is going on.

Television is 'real' because it is in picture form and, as human beings, we react to the visual impact of real people in real time.

Many people find period drama more acceptable and entertaining. That is not necessarily because of the lack of bad language (a sweet release in itself) but more because the visual impact of period costume immediately tells the subconscious that **this is not today**. It is **not happening now** and it does not relate to the modern experience.

PERSONAL PERSPECTIVE

Many people had the same reaction when **watching the refugees** coming out of Kosovo in news items. They were a people detached from our society because they were dressed in **peasant clothes** that seemed to relate to another era and another culture.

But how stark was the reaction when, suddenly, those who were on our screens pouring over the Albanian border were wearing **exactly the same clothes as our children wear**. Exactly the same style of clothing that we would put on. Indeed, the reaction then is, "this is happening to people **just like me.**"

The power of the media drives the population in all manner of directions. Those who control the media, to a large degree control our lives and the way that we react. And they know it.

It **is safe** to travel on buses, it **is safe** for our children to travel on their own, to walk or to cycle to school. Cycling is as **safe as it has ever been, or even**

21

safer, because of the helmets, guards, lights, safety bands and so on that all exist today in our society, if people would wear them.

The OECD research recently released declared Great Britain as the safest country in Europe for children after Sweden. The safest; and the most paranoid.

The tragedy of accidents and impromptu aggressive or antisocial acts will always be with society no matter what we do. A senior constable in a substantial township once explained, **"we know the 317 people who create 95% of the crime in this town, and if we could lock them all up there would be very little need for my police force** in respect of petty crime, burglary, car theft and so on."

"But," he said, **"you just can't lock people up**, can you?"

And I guess you can't.

If our politicians react to the problems of 'Deirdre'-type incidents born of a fiction, bigger than most of us could ever imagine, what chance has society as a whole of conducting itself in a rational fashion? What trust can one have in the politicians' utterances if they exhibit that level of influence from the media?

THE COMPLIANT ARE THE VICTIMS

The **naughty, the ill-mannered, disruptive child** will 'win' the attention of their very own, **one-to-one, teacher** in today's society. The media sees to that.

The well-mannered, tolerant child who has difficulty 'keeping up' will merely be allowed to settle into the relative obscurity of their class, to slowly sink inexorably to the lower reaches of the rankings. In short, our society **penalises the real victim**. The real victim is the conformist. Ultimately the victim is the teacher who witnesses the coercive pressures.

CHAPTER 4

OWN GOALS ARE TOO COMMON

The consumerist lobby must have been proud of itself when, at the end of the millennium year, in a state of euphoria because they had succeeded in convincing the United Kingdom Government that costs could be contained in life assurance companies and cheap cars could be obtained by buying from foreign dealerships, the Equitable Life, the bastion of non-commission paying philanthropy, stopped taking on new business.

THE CONSUMERISTS ARE PROFITEERING

Daewoo Corp. declared the group 'insolvent', with massive debts. Vauxhall and Ford made known their intention to close Luton and part of Dagenham car manufacturing plants. And, yes, of course, the pièce de résistance was BMW.

BMW sold Rover for £10.00.

One can almost see old man Steptoe saying to his son:

"Oh 'arold, when are you ever going to start paying attention to your dear old dad? You knows you've got to get out on the cart."

Of course, the modern day 'rider' to that statement would be:

" 'cos you knows there's a **field full of new Rovers being sold orf for scrap value.**"

Profiteering, millennium-style, it seems, is the **art of losing £2m a day** and having a spokesperson for the consumer who does not even understand the basic principles of commerce. Is it a matter of bad management or bad work force? Is it a matter of poor communications and misinformation? Or could it be that the desire to survive at any cost and become the 'big cheese' overshadows good business practice?

Sheila McKecknie must be very pleased that for once in her association's history, she can confirm its proper membership numbers, even though her organisation still 'cannot spare staff time to answer letters about misinformation in 'Which?' magazine'.

As a business the Consumer Association 'votes' commodities and services in and out of favour with the deftness of Julius Caesar on a good day at the 'games'. Dyson with other people's lives some would call it. Others just fail to see the 'sickness' of the joke.

CULINARY CLEANLINESS

The latest **'victim'** of regulatory **political correctness** is **Clarissa Dixon Wright**, recently criticised by the **Chartered Institute of Environmental Health** as having 'sloppy' habits and 'risking' spreading germs. Tut, tut, I mean licking fingers and then plunging them into unprepared food. How terrible. No one in their own house would do that of course.

Raw meat and vegetables on the same chopping board. Mmmm. Is there no end to the misery and suffering of the British public? The offending utensil would be a **wooden** chopping board, of course.

Clarissa is of course the remaining TV cookery personality from the '*Two Fat Ladies*' duo, and love them or hate them they provided good entertainment, down-to-earth cooking, and were advocates for the devouring of the odd bit of 'dirt'. We can be over-sensitive.

We all appreciate that E-coli bacteria can kill, but then so can a lot of other things, like being hit by a number 12 omnibus.

One suspects that the **BBC will succumb** to the formal complaint and the 'institute' will chalk up yet another "success". But one wonders who the success is for; themselves or a nation that will become so isolated from natural contamination that it will become like the chick, that grows into the pullet, that lays the egg, that has the salmonella in it. **The chicks need to peck muck to reduce the salmonella bacteria that live in their gut.**

Nature will have its way. We are an animal like any other animal. Whilst we should not go out of our way to be unhygienic, there is a balance that it is **for the individual to strike** on occasions, rather than officialdom.

Surely we do have the sense to see whether Clarissa or any other TV personality is **going over the top** in their lack of hygiene. Are these lapses in culinary hygiene any worse for society than the constant, unrelenting **diet of bad language and sexual innuendo that we endure?** Do they all have a shower 'before and after'?

Responsibility sits with the person or corporation that makes the decision.

If responsibility was taken to its logical conclusion today there would be a lot of politicians who would be living in poverty to match those whom they have disaffected over the past years in various parts of our society. Civil servants and local officials should be responsible for their actions. Society pays them to do a good job and they should deliver it without excuses.

I can hear old man Steptoe now,

"Yeah, you big Jessie, a bit of muck won't 'urt ya."

The professional 'muck slingers' know just how much it can hurt though, don't they?

HAPHAZARD HYGIENE

Common sense should tell us we need a bit of the right kind of muck. Every other animal species, and a lot of our own for that matter, seem to live very well without the over-burdening prescriptive nonsense that Harold and his dad seem to argue about so often.

"In my day..."

"In your day," 'arold would retort, "vey didn't know what hygiene was. Look at you, you dirty old man."

Of course, the series always used to come up with at least one occasion when this 'dirty old man' got cleaned up and really shone. And, of course, modern society does not want to live in a dustbin. But, hey, maybe that is what happiness is all about.

Are 'arold and Mr. Steptoe really just figments of somebody's imagination? No. There are thousands, probably millions of 'Steptoe & Sons', which certain parts of society would not only denigrate perforce but would **lord over because, well, they know what is best for 'that kind of person'**.

I mean to say, what could Harold and old man Steptoe possibly know, they are only **rag-and-bone-men** with no experience of real life. What order, discipline, or financial and political awareness can 'that type' of individual really deliver to the intellectually astute?

But, of course, **Harold is intellectually astute**. That is part of his character, with his pseudo-refined voice and predisposition to 'put it on' on occasions, he contrasts very well with his father who has only life's experience to draw on whereas, of course, Harold has had an education and reads books.

Harold epitomises the consumerist. The demeaning task of clip-clopping round the streets collecting 'tat' and recycling rubbish is something that a more organised and somehow refined system should achieve in a different fashion.

The fact that a horse and cart are cost-effective and that Harold meets his own overheads and scrapes a living for his dad and himself seem irrelevant.

They do, of course, take all of the financial risk and provide some 'colour' on the streets of their particular city, which goes firmly against those who want to spend millions of pounds setting up a formal mechanism that costs a fortune to run and constitutes a bureaucratic nightmare to control.

PRACTICAL COMMERCE IS CHILD'S PLAY

Bottles used to be collected by children and taken back to the store where glass was exchanged for money. Money was spent on sweets. The glass was returned to the original manufacturer, **delivery lorries were full in both directions,** 'outward' with goods, 'backwards' with empties.

Now we have bottle banks, cluttering up some of our most picturesque views, the contents of which are collected by special lorries that go out empty and come back full, passing the delivery lorries with full bottles on board, going out full and returning empty. **So much for bureaucratic intelligence and a reduction in environmental hazards.**

Legislation does not solve these problems, commercial activity does. Not money. **Anyone with the resources can throw money at a problem. Government**s of every hue are renowned for their expertise in this practice.

Commercial activity operates at the very lowest level. It allows those with the most meagre of resources to eke out a living. Like the unemployed individual who was murdered because he confided in a friend that he earned thousands of pounds from selling 'Big Issue', sometimes you are best keeping 'mum' about your successes because others get avaricious.

The beggars on London streets earning over £100 a day pay no more tax than the inspired individual who would collect bottles or tins (or any other commodity) that has a recycling price. The entrepreneur would deliver the 'product' to the appropriate centre for redistribution.

Of course, supermarkets 'cannot cope' with having to take bottles back and return tins. Small shopkeepers were quite happy to do it. It was part of what they did to fill in time when they were not filling shelves and serving people.

Perhaps we should reflect more kindly on 'Mr Steptoe' with his wrinkled face, uneven teeth and ill-kempt appearance and remember those somewhat immortal words that he uttered "now, in my day..."; **perhaps history can teach us more than we give it credit for.**

A MARGIN IS ESSENTIAL

Government ministers might do better acknowledging 'small business' for what it is, innovative, risk taking, self-financing, as opposed to tax evading, pernicious and parasitic, whilst also acknowledging that larger businesses have their place, each is interdependent upon the other.

Dictating margins at either extreme or, for that matter, in between, can only be detrimental to the consumer in the long run.

Fields full of cars that have resulted from over-production have to be sold to give way to new models. It is worth reflecting once again that **forty years of the Austin Mini failed to earn its manufacturer a penny piece during its extended lifetime.** Perhaps it is time to get back to proper commercial principles and dump consumerism for what it is; an expensive, ill-informed and, one has to say, elitist source of gross misinformation.

And what about the other waste of course:

" 'arold! have you mucked your 'orse out yet?'

I mean, what happened to <u>that</u> waste?

Well, people used to walk round and collect a bag of it and take it back and put it around the roses. And it was not 90% straw either. It was good, rose-growing, horse muck. Not something that people had to get into their car and drive to a supermarket or garden centre to buy in a bottle. A natural waste product that beats diesel fumes any day.

A skit on a *Which?* report on chemicals that illustrates the ability that exists to defame even the most common of substances.

WATER – A VERY DANGEROUS AND CORROSIVE NECESSITY

FOR LIFE.

CAUTION - DANGEROUS LIQUID

Corrosive to most metals
Dangerous at high and low temperatures
Can be fatal if inhaled
Damaging to paper, fabrics and wood
May contain poisonous organisms
Can have diuretic effect if swallowed
Avoid prolonged exposure to skin
Hazardous to traffic
Can induce strange psychological effects in warm weather.
(Many people tend to take their clothes off when near it)

Some of society's perceptions can be exposed for the myths that they are.

CHAPTER 5

A TRAFFIC-CALMING EXPERIENCE

Locals know the way to get round traffic jams, obstacles and major hold-ups, which actually eases congestion rather than creating it. They use 'rat runs'.

The Local Authorities' answer to that knowledge is to place miniaturised and extended **'sleeping policemen'** at strategic distances down a length of road, so that a car is forced to slow down to 5-10 miles an hour or suffer the consequences of an expensive garage bill, to then accelerate away throwing up to **twenty times as much pollution into the air** as the car would have done had it been allowed to travel at normal speed for the length of the road without the impediment in its way.

The Local Authorities have not only seen fit to put humps in the road but they have also invested in some **'low speed' chicanes**. The City Engineer had obviously never ridden on a bus (one has some doubts as to whether they ever get on anything other than a bike).

Jim is a bus driver. He drives one of these new low-level 'green diesel', **environmentally-friendly buses** that ensures that the disabled can hop on and off without any problems. Also, of course, the elderly who have trouble getting up high steps find the buses better for access.

ENVIRONMENTALLY FRIENDLY

Jim loves his new bus and, of course, they are a great British innovation. Big windows, good views. Excellent for passengers.

Now Maizie was a regular traveller on the buses. She was quite pleased with the new bus as well. Coming in from Lower Feltham it made a great change not to have to struggle to almost jump up off the footpath to get on board.

31

Jim greeted her with a smile, checked her bus pass and took her reduced fare ticket.

It was one of those sort of days; the sky was blue, but occasionally it would cloud over. Not a day to get depressed about, you understand, but one that Maizie might complain about if it deteriorated any further. Mind you, she did not like it too hot either.

As they approached the centre of the township Jim admired the newly finished road ahead of him.

The council had taken several months digging up the whole of the centre of the High Street to put in block paving and speed ramps to stop the cars going through too fast. **The council had also added a new special bus lane**, gouged out in a special channel that only buses could use. He brought his new vehicle in to the left believing that when he parked at the bus stop and opened the door, Maizie would not have to 'step' anywhere. It would be just as if it was a flat continuous surface between bus floor and pavement.

Jim was an experienced driver. Turning into this new lower road section he got a funny feeling that something was not really quite right.

The long single-decker bus quickly produced evidence of the fact that the engineers who had designed this piece of road sculpture had failed to run a model bus through their model figures. Jim's bus came to a very uncomfortable halt.

RESPONSIBILITY FOR OFFICIALDOM'S MISTAKES

The **bus tried to mount the pavement** but, of course, the kerb was a little bit too high, having been raised to be at the same level as the bus's loading platform. The wheels were at a difficult angle due to the turning attitude required for the 'swish' movement that would normally precede the designed stop; parallel to the kerb.

Discretion being the better part of valour, Jim backed out. "Don't worry, my dear, we will get you off," he said to Maizie, "just a technical hitch," and the beeping of the reversing alarm was an indicator to Maizie to regain her seat. "Never been on a bus going backwards," she thought. A completely new experience for her.

By now the bus was pointing across the middle of Feltham High Street, in front of it the new traffic ramp, designed to slow the cars, which had no real alternative route, as they passed through. Jim had to press on, his timetable was running behind and his bus charged forward, slowly of course, over the ramp.

The bus was a 'low-level' bus designed to help the disabled and elderly to gain access. What such low-slung machines are **not designed** to do is to go over **traffic humps**.

It is going to cost £ millions to take out all of the traffic humps that are on new low-level 'disabled and elderly-friendly' bus routes because, as Jim found out to his employer's cost, when he got stuck astride Feltham's new version of Mount Everest, the humps are just too tall for this sort of vehicle.

The crunching sound from underneath Jim's bus just had to be heard to be believed. Maizie let out a startled cry, Jim was most upset and all the other passengers were panicking because now, of course, their unloading platform was probably twice as high from the ground as it would have been at a normal kerb. **How on earth were they going to get off this rather exaggerated see-saw?**

Jim's question of Maizie might be one that would have been asked by anybody in the circumstances or indeed standing outside:

How on earth did a **local authority engineer** ever get to the point of employing people to construct a totally **inappropriate facility** at a cost of probably half a million pounds in a busy High Street?

A complete reconstruction of the road was required. **Who was going to pay?**

Well, if you lived anywhere closely associated with the locality, **the answer was; you.**

It would surely have been more beneficial to have created the environment and **tested** it with buses of the appropriate design **before** shifting into high gear and **doing the work.**

IT'S A MATTER OF ADJUSTMENT

Most people these days realise that all buses in rural areas are front-end loaders. This is largely because **there are no conductors and the driver has to take the fares.** Bert, like Jim, was well used to driving his bus. He had been on the Skegness route for a number of years.

The buses were modern and a great initiative by the County Council and bus companies for an hourly bus service between Lincoln and Skegness, meeting up with smaller bus services that may be operated by a taxi service at locations along the way to form a service called 'Connect'.

The road transport engineers thought that they should perhaps help the 'Connect' service out **by encouraging more disabled and elderly** to use the bus and avoid the high-step problem that we already looked at with Jim's circumstances.

The authority set out to double the height of the kerb by creating a sort of **flat-topped mound** as part of the pavement, adjacent to which the bus platform would be at the same level and facilitate easy access and egress from the bus.

New bus shelters would also be put in, sympathetic to the local rural environment to allow people to stay out of the bad weather whilst waiting for their bus to arrive. A great incentive for people to use the bus and a good initiative for the local authority to pursue.

RAMPANT MODIFICATIONS TO 'BUS STOPS'

Bert's first journey after they had finished modifications in one of the villages and the outlying lay-bys on the main road could not have been more full of surprises.

In the middle of Langworth village the pavement had been raised **and Bert could slide his bus neatly alongside to allow his passengers on and off.** It could not work better.

The next bus stop in Sudbrooke was in a lay-by; Bert saw passengers waiting next to the bus shelter, which was at the far end of the bus pull-in. Imagine his consternation when swinging in as he passed the heightened kerb, and finally came to rest with his front door adjacent to the shelter and **his rear wheel adjacent to the modified pavement.**

Maybe they are planning to run double-deckers with central doors again he thought; and put conductors on them for good measure. I suppose it could have been put in for the few enthusiasts of the Lincoln Vintage Vehicle Society who might run their buses along the route once a year. It was certainly of little help to Bert or his passengers on this occasion. **The bus company had not operated rear-door buses for 30 years.**

He drove on to the next 'stop', which was again a lay-by next to a busy junction and had a traffic island opposite it. Fortunately they had not placed a raised pavement into this facility, but as he drew up to the bus shelter at the far end of the lay-by Bert was able to note another useful addition to the kerb-edge profile.

The council had put a 'dropped' kerb precisely where the loading platform for the bus came to rest. The dropped kerb was to facilitate the disabled and elderly getting across from the traffic island, but, of course, the facility made it even more difficult for those passengers to step up into their awaiting transport.

35

Bert got back to the garage and reflected with one of his mates, "It is really not worth going on holiday, you know, you never know what is going to be in store for you when you get back, do you?"

CONGESTION IN THE COUNTRYSIDE – BY DESIGN

Like so many facilities that are put in to assist those in our society who have major or minor disabilities, and like the traffic engineers in **Leicester** who decided to **create congestion outside of the city** so that they would not get congestion in it, a little thought would go a long way. Very often the 'idea' is implemented without proper research being carried out.

And what happens to the errant genius that puts all these schemes in? Well, it seems he is promoted, suspended on full pay, or probably retired because of stress with his **pension enhanced by six years**, so that the public can still continue to pay for him until they **eventually put him into a box.**

The problem is, the earlier they retire the longer they seem to live. **A 'lose, lose' situation** if ever one came across one.

Now the word is out that 500,000 'sleeping policemen' style road-calming devices are to be removed or lowered because the new generation buses (designed specifically for these routes) will 'ground' on the existing obstacles. Who pays for the ineptness; the lack of cohesive foresight? YOU.

THE POLITICIANS WILL BRUSH THE HUNDREDS OF THOUSANDS OF POUNDS ASIDE.

The **political expediency** of ill-prepared experimentation, even in the face of contrary evidence given before the speed restrictive mechanisms were put in place, will just be another 'one of those things' that you, **the public**, put up with and **pay for.**

PERCEPTIONS RULE 'OK'

Noel Coward wrote plays from his observations. Dickens did much the same. But when you get into the **local politics** of 'sleeping policemen' and 'traffic-calming' devices, the only thing that you could truly write, with any sincerity, is **a Brian Rix farce.**

The one thing that is observed is that **millions of pounds** of public money is spent each year on **dealing with perception**. "Do not confuse me with the facts, it is what I perceive that is the truth."

"Traffic goes through here at 60 miles an hour." Quote: local resident who has difficulty crossing the road. (He only moved into the village last year.)

A police check reveals that the average speed of cars going through the village is 36 miles an hour instead of the prescribed 30. Far-fetched? Not at all. The figures and statements reflect genuine case histories. The solution? Roadside cameras. How do we know? Because the police monitor them and their effectiveness.

Very often what we perceive is not representative of the **facts of the matter**.

Should we be concerned about the facts of the matter? Surely, even cars going an average of 6 miles an hour above the limit is rather too much for the local population to have to bear isn't it?

But is the remedy to make the road surface a multicoloured network of red, green, grey and white lines that, **allegedly, encourage motorists to slow down?**

Observe the now enlarged speed restriction signs complete with the red and white "large square" backdrop. These have to be the perfect mechanism to stop motorists from driving into the **bollards** (or safety islands) which are carefully constructed at strategic distances on our more generously wide thoroughfares to force head-on collisions with the odd ambulance or fire engine (not to mention police vehicles) when they are obliged to use the 'wrong side' of the road in an emergency.

Parked cars at kerb sides **are a proven mechanism for slowing traffic** speeds. The great thing about parked cars on the streets of a town or a city is that the cars arrive in the morning as traffic builds up. The drivers are accommodated for the duration of their visit whilst the vehicle, at no cost, retards traffic speeds by constriction.

In the evening, when there is less traffic, the highways become wide and unimpeded. Bollards fail to achieve much, even it seems for pedestrians at most sites.

MINI 'ISLANDS' – ALL THE RAGE

The appearance of mini-roundabouts which have been suitably placed to join "Enderby Crescent", that 'minor road', with a sixth of the traffic of the 'major road' with which it connects, IS LIKE A RASH OF MEASLES: AND ALMOST AS DEADLY.

The scheme may or may not calm traffic. **It certainly succeeds in enraging motorists.** And, it appears, increases the accident rate at, or adjacent to, the site.

That is not to say that all 'traffic calming' is bad. It is not to say that you are against public expenditure that will safeguard human and material loss. One could on occasion be forgiven for asking whether the road markings **always indicate to all road users** precisely what should be happening or **what action they should be taking.**

"The local residents reported at a public meeting that they were being continually drawn from their houses to sweep up glass and console those whose material damage was plain to see and whose emotional distress was totally unnecessary. This was **an experiment** that neither the local police nor the local authority monitored. **The mini-roundabout had cost £38,000 to put in and a similar amount to remove.** The local authority used every trick in the book, apart from solid statistical facts, to retain it."

It was only the local Chamber of Commerce and an ever-compliant band of frustrated motorists that succeeded in bringing common sense to bear.

Unfortunately, this is not an isolated story. A similar scheme in a similar village went through much the same tortuous and unnecessary hiatus. The evidence is countrywide. The cost is horrendous.

Of course, the people who have benefited are **those who paint** multicoloured road markings and put down white lines. They must be **laughing all the way to the bank**. More important local issues remain impoverished through a lack of funds.

Local politicians justify their position because, of course, the Parish Council requested the traffic calming in the first place. On what basis? On the back of a perception without adequate investigation. A few facts and a need to win some 'brownie points' for a local election here or there seem to be sufficient to 'win the day'. Some decisions can only be described as squalid.

MINORITY RULE

Two members of the public attended a county engineers' meeting at a village hall to decide the fate of a proposed local by-pass. The two attendees voted against the by-pass and it was lost, for ever. How intellectually talented does one have to be to know that the attendance was not representative of the local population?

Surely we should have a more scientific mechanism to determine how large amounts of money are spent? One can conclude that the local authorities are deliberately avoiding repairs to roads so that they can save the expense of putting in 'sleeping policemen'.

The ruts in the road, developed by lack of maintenance, act in much the same way as manufactured 'mounds' and perversely improve the road accident figures by slowing traffic down to such an extent that it creates congestion.

This adds to that second, manifestly obtuse, concern of local authorities and Government, air pollution from exhaust emissions. The topic should herald a new chapter, and it does.

CHAPTER 6

CONGESTION AND ENVIRONMENTAL HAZARDS

The way to deal with emissions is to follow the lead of Leicester City Council. Leicester Councillors are actually going to create congestion **outside the city**, we are told in an authoritatively explicit article in the *Daily Telegraph*.

By **keeping pollution in the countryside** they will persuade motorists, because of long tailbacks and traffic queues, to use public transport as an alternative to their own vehicles!

Which planet do these 'experts' come from? Oh no, this is not an April 1st joke, this is **somebody's serious thought on how to deal with traffic pollution in a major city.** Of course, the whole commuting and commercial (those buying from Leicester businesses) communities will be firmly behind **this great initiative** to improve their environment; to lose trade and employment opportunities to other less adventurous cities.

Businesses do not 'serve' themselves in isolation. They serve the public. If that trading public moves, so, eventually, will the businesses.

SLOWING DOWN TRAFFIC SPEEDS UP POLLUTION

It never seems to dawn on traffic engineers or politicians that placing **traffic lights every thirty yards** and bringing the flow of traffic to a grinding halt **increases pollutio**n. In fact, in the 1990s one was witnessing a game of political 'bribery' between local Government and the national budgets.

The Government set a national transport strategy against which the local authorities had to 'lodge' a bid document.
The more bizarre ideas that one could use to convince national Government that your plan was 'in line' with theirs, the more chance there was of

41

obtaining funding for genuine local requirements. Local policy was, and still is, dictated by a remote bureaucracy that holds the purse strings.

What would you do at a roundabout like this?

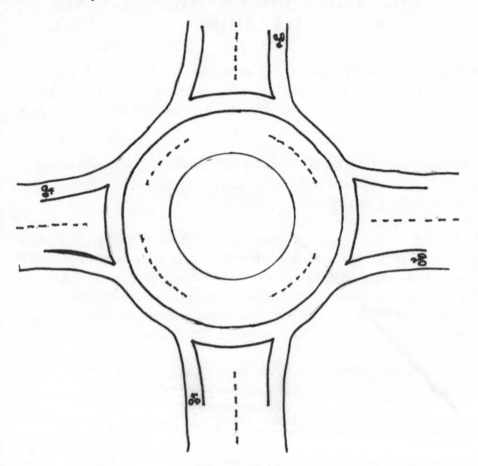

Is there anything in the Highway Code that relates to this set of road markings? Could it be the result of an hallucination or is it just an attempt to raise more money from Government because the council want **to be seen to be doing something to help cyclists**?

Does it help cyclists? "Time to go to bed," said Florence.

"Boing," said Zebedee.

It has escaped the Department of Transport's notice that this road configuration was popular in Holland until the 1980s. It was discontinued because of the huge number of fatal accidents where cyclists, declaring their right of way, jousted with motorists in a 'no win' situation.

Why wasn't somebody asking for the facts? Why wasn't somebody saying to a nation of cycling heritage "what could we do to improve the lot of cyclists on British roads, that you have tried and found successful, and what shouldn't we do that you have found endangered life?"

Coincidentally most cyclists have no lights during the hours of darkness. The majority STILL ride on the pavements. Few wear any form of head protection or 'visibility' clothing. Are the priorities right?

MONITORING PROGRESS? NOT IF YOU'RE POOR

Does the **County Council** monitor these experimental road markings? Not at all. They state that they **cannot afford** to monitor schemes.

The cost of putting the lines on the road amounts to hundreds of thousands of pounds. The distraction to motorists is palpable. Two lanes of traffic have been reduced to one, congestion has been increased severalfold. It is an exponential problem. The worse you make it, the worse it gets. And **the authorities do not check the scheme's effectiveness.**

Emissions increase at a rate broadly similar to the motorist's blood pressure.

Perhaps the answer is to make the bureaucrats, particularly **local authority officials, personally responsible for those schemes that they get wrong**. Those that they get right, they can earn a bonus for. The cynic glories in the thought that the bonuses will be very small on current performance.

What the red tarmac, or in some places grey; others green, has done is reduce two useful lanes of traffic, one turning left, the other 'going straight on or turning right', to one lane of traffic which is going in all directions. **The 'innovation' actually makes matters worse for cyclists, and the long-suffering motorist**.

Neither the ambulance service nor the police keep comprehensive records of where accidents happen, what happens, what the injuries are, in a form that can easily be analysed.

One would not wish to add to the bureaucracy that is an impediment to their already overburdened resources. But, you would have thought, wouldn't you, that having that information would be part and parcel of dealing with road traffic management?

Facts only get in the way of what is needed to satisfy public perception that **politicians are actually doing something.**

AN ELECTRONICALLY CONTROLLED GYRATORY TRAFFIC SYSTEM

Whilst on the subject of roundabouts (islands), how about this for a 'roundabout' that is not a roundabout, this manifestation of a fertile imagination conspires to **combine 'cycle art' with traffic light excesses.**

This is **Lincoln's infamous 'Magic Roundabout'**. It is actually **"an electronically controlled gyratory system"**. It only requires 'Dougal' 'Florence' and 'Zebedee' to make it complete.

It only looks like a roundabout. It is huge.

At each traffic light the system gathers **'platoons' of cars** (and that should tell you something of the mentality of the person who designed it) to then be 'discharged' into a 'controlled' area where all of the traffic lights change sequentially. If it is a good day, the 'scoot' system will move the 'platoon' a whole 150 yards, in a smooth, if frantic, surge of momentary activity.

Children, adults, drivers and pedestrians have all raised the question of Lincoln's 'Magic Roundabout'; **why the traffic signals cannot be switched off or be 'part-time'.**

The political reply?

It is an **'electronically controlled gyratory system'** not a roundabout. "The angle at which the roads join does not allow the traffic lights to be switched off because the junction would become too hazardous."

However, one can compare it to any number of other road layouts in or around other cities (A47 Kings Lynn, the Chiswick flyover, West London; examples abound) and indeed examples in the same city, which operate in a very efficient manner without traffic lights. Free-flowing traffic is achieved with the same road-angling of entry and egress as this 'Magic Roundabout' and much larger volumes of traffic.

TRAVEL BY TRAIN

Perhaps we should abandon the car for public transport; after all 'trains travel on Sundays'.

The journey by car would have been just an hour and a half. If traffic was bad it could be two hours. However, the return trip of between three and four hours was rather daunting, even though the dubious effervescent company of our son for at least half of that time, as he was transported from Lincoln to Derby, was perhaps worth some of the inconvenience.

But there were environmental issues. There were cost issues, too. Using the car, when a "good public system of transport" was available, seemed to be a bad use of resources. Doing something for the 'green' issues was a useful by-product.

The train fare was also a consideration; £9.00 instead of probably £19.00 plus of course, the wear and tear on the car (not to mention an aging parent). What the hell, we decided we were going for it, **train travel or bust**.

Travel on a Sunday between places of major interest, on a major rail-link connecting the Midlands and seaside resorts of some renown is not like going from one unknown place to another. **There had to be** 'early in the day' links between Derby and Nottingham, Loughborough, or Leicester and Cleethorpes or Skegness, with all the attractions; so that people could spend a full day at their destination. And, of course, **what goes east, must go west** and bring people back through the city of Lincoln.

It might even bring people holidaying in Cleethorpes 'inland' for the day. It is only a forty-five minute trip on the train to the historic city with panoramic **views of the castle, cathedral and the dramatic inland attraction** of the Roman port in the centre of Lincoln; the Brayford Pool. The train might carry people from Lincoln through to Newark, another historical town with excellent shopping facilities and a history centred on the Cromwellian/Royalist conflicts of the Middle Ages.

Nottingham, of course, is an attraction in its own right with links with Robin Hood, a huge castle and so on. Two-way traffic to attractive destinations surely meant **plenty of trains and a good degree of choice?**

The timetable would illustrate the times of trains.

There is a somewhat flawed logic in that statement.

The timetable, unfortunately, did not cover the complete journey from Lincoln to Derby, even though it was known that trains oftentimes did, the complete journey, that is. The timetable indicated trains as far as Nottingham and **then a separate timetable was required** to continue the journey.

"Ah, here we are, mid-morning train 11.00am. Ah no, it only goes as far as Newark Northgate. That is obviously to connect into the main line trains north:south. It was just a pity we did not want to be at either King's Cross or Edinburgh."

46

Within that brief passage of time the timetable was whisked away, and mother was already on the phone **dialling the 'freephone' number from the back cover of the timetable.**

> "Lincoln to Derby please, mid-morning Sunday." The deftness of her hand moving swiftly with the pen over a small square pad of clear white paper indicated that this was a journey of some complexity.

> "11.00, just to Newark. Grantham, yes. Change Nottingham, yes, arrive Derby 14.33, yes thank you," and she hung up.

There is **only one connecting train before mid-afternoon**: and **that does not connect!** The journey is Newark/Grantham/Nottingham/Derby and it takes three and a half hours.

"Walking is environmentally friendly," suggested father. The observation was ignored.

The astonishment and disenchantment of the possibility of several changes of train accompanied by **long spells on deserted railway platforms prompted the offer of an anorak and notepad.** This was not quite what the potential passenger had in mind. But he would go with it; the dislocated journey, that is, not the distinctive wearing apparel.

He had a return ticket and the journey was not really too bad, was it?

There was a later train, mother had ascertained, but that went via Wakefield and the journey time was only four hours and five minutes, again changing at Newark. Instead of going south on the high-speed GNER rail-link, the journey would go north.

It was at this point that memories of a previous journey, to Derby via Sheffield, were recalled.

> "I had to **pay an excess fare** on that trip, which just about doubled the price," the boy spluttered.

When the situation was queried with the ticket inspector, sorry, customer relations manager, he had replied:

> "Well **what else can you expect, you are travelling a lot further** than you would have done had you gone direct from Lincoln to Derby via Nottingham."

That was apparent to 'the lad' before he had ever set foot on the train and, of course, this was the only route available to get him from Lincoln to Derby that the railway system could offer.

The extra mileage could have the same consequences on the prospective journey going via Grantham, although probably less costly than going via Wakefield which, because it was even further around than the Sheffield route, was likely to **result in a fare that was three times the original**. The Wakefield route was not really an option.

Mother stepped in once more.

> "Let's take him to Grantham in the car, it is only an hour's drive,"

and mother was back on the phone again.

> "Trains from Grantham to Derby please."

Now this route was on the Skegness/Midlands line and there did seem to be a few more trains from Grantham: 11.03, 11.57, 12.33 etc. and the journey times were good.

A résumé running through father's head was:

> an hour's drive from home in Lincoln to Grantham and, of course, the return trip, then, a further hour and a half on the railway.

"But you can use the ticket that you have already have. If you caught the train in Lincoln it would be going via Grantham anyway," said father learnedly.

Learnedly? Father had not thought it through, but the lad had.

"But dad, they will probably charge me an excess fare because Grantham is not on the normal route from Lincoln to Derby, is it?"

Oh, this was far too much for dad.

"I'll tell you what," father said, "I'll drive you to Derby after church on Sunday, it will certainly be quicker, and it will probably be cheaper.

I don't believe all this environmental tosh anyway. **One good volcanic eruption chucks more environmentally-unfriendly 'crud' into the atmosphere than all the cars that man has ever invented**, I will just put these timetables back in the drawer."

CHAPTER 7

POLITICAL INSTANT REACTIONS

Politicians seldom seem to wait to see 'the problem' for what the problem actually is.

Take Concorde. The full horror of a flying blowtorch was manifested in the media and generated the usual wave of panic and speculation. Instead of waiting for the Board of Enquiry or even the initial enquiry to finish, every newspaper in the land had three and four pages of 'It did this, and it did that,' but what exactly did 'it' do? Nobody knew.

Let's speculate: as everyone else does.

Seemingly, and by an incredible chance of fate, a 17" metal strip, from an aircraft that had previously used the runway, dug into one of the Concorde's tyres causing it to burst. The tyre 'exploded'.

Either the metal strip or fragments of the tyre were thrown up into the underside of the wing, which punctured the starboard fuel tanks. The aircraft was fully laden with fuel, taking 'once in a lifetime' travellers for the aircraft experience of the twentieth century. Supersonic flight.

GETTING TO THE ROOT CAUSE

The subsequent blowtorch effect was at once spectacular and horrific. Charles de Gaulle airport was the centre of media attention and speculation as fuel from the ruptured tank spewed into the flame and intense heat of the powerful 'afterburners' of the engine efflux.

But the fire was a manifestation of the problem: it was not the problem.

The fire could have burnt all day because it was burning behind the aeroplane. Concorde uses afterburners, which produce a very hot and

51

extended flame behind the aircraft, which, under normal circumstances, is quite harmless to the aircraft.

Harmless though it may be, in the circumstances that pertained to the stricken Concorde, when gallons of fuel (litres for those who are interested in metrication) fall into the path of a naked flame they tend to ignite, and that is probably what happened. Something ignited the fuel.

But the ignition happened **behind the aeroplane**. Therefore, if it was just the fire that was in contention the aeroplane could well have stayed in the air, completed a 'circuit' of the airport and landed, or diverted to another airfield.

The problem, however, was the loss of fuel. Fuel is heavy. If a carefully balanced aircraft loses weight on one side and maintains weight on the opposite side then the aeroplane loses its ability to fly straight and level.

The heavy weight on the port side of the aeroplane will force it over into a roll; no matter what the pilot tries to do or how effective fire extinguishers might be. The accident was a tragic consequence of a circumstance beyond anybody's control. So why was Concorde grounded?

British Concordes have guards to avoid 'things' being thrown up into the wing, French Concordes, apparently, did not.

It now appears that the politicians decide when commercial aeroplanes will fly and when they won't, despite the fact that it deprives thousands of people of an experience that they may perhaps wait half a lifetime to fulfil and may well be denied for ever. There are a limited number of aeroplanes with a limited number of seats and a limited number of flights that they can make.

TAKING RESPONSIBILITY FOR RISK

Apparently an individual can set off in a yacht to sail round the world and have millions of pounds expended on trying to find them when radio communication is lost. People can take the choice of climbing Kilimanjaro or Everest, of even walking in the 'fells' and have hundreds of thousands of pounds spent recovering their remains when the gamble goes wrong.

Or worse still, other people's lives are put at risk whilst attempting to rescue you from your own folly.

Yet politicians deem us so inadequately imbued with intelligence that having established that a high-profile aeroplane was the subject of a chance catastrophic experience, thousands will be denied the ability to make a personal choice on whether their personal 'risk' is 'worth' the experience.

Or could it be that some politicians somewhere were fearful of the fact that not fitting guards to French aircraft was a bureaucrat's decision? Time may tell – but the cover-ups are usually very well camouflaged.

If the aircraft had been a Boeing 737 or an Airbus subject to exactly the same criteria, would the 'fleet' have been grounded?

Yet bureaucrats somewhere, somehow, decide that because **the media** immediately **created "the death knell" of Concorde**, keeping the aeroplane on the ground was the safest option for the flying public. It is certainly safe. You cannot crash if you don't take off, although even that myth was quashed when two 'Jumbo Jets' collided in Tenerife.

Plaything of the wealthy? There are thousands of people who save for years to take that one exciting flight on Concorde. It is the prized and treasured birthday gift or anniversary present that many people treasure above all else.

The commercial effect on the airlines is also very damaging. Concorde cannot earn revenue standing on the tarmac. Any modifications to the fuel tanks or reinforcement to the underwing structure could have been dealt with over a period of time in line with scheduled servicing procedures.

Our endless ability to denigrate that which is good; to undermine that which is interesting and exciting to ordinary individuals, and to thwart the endeavours of those who merely seek to live an uncontentious life, doing something that harms nobody else, is really beyond belief.

53

There have, apparently, been 57 burst tyres on Concorde aircraft, 30 on Air France-operated aircraft. Six of those 57 resulted in fuel tank punctures. Of course there may be wider issues, but they are probably unconnected to the tragedy.

Is it reasonable to assume that that is what has taken place?

HOW SAFE IS SAFE?

Using the tyre as a metaphor, those of us who drive cars or ride cycles have no doubt experienced a puncture at some time or other; but how many of us have actually **experienced an explosive blow out**?

An explosive blow out is where the tyre deflates very quickly and shreds into pieces. It does happen.

The Air France Concorde flight taking off from Charles De Gaulle airport started off as an ordinary mundane flight and turned into a tragedy which cost one hundred and thirteen lives. The reason? An explosive blow out.

The chances of it happening in the way it did are probably millions to one. But they happen. Does that stop us relying on tyres as a mechanism for safety, smoothness, comfort, directional control and so on?

There was a **similar tragedy** in America, which cost **twenty-three British tourists' lives**. The bus in which they were travelling had an explosive 'blow out' of one of its tyres, the driver lost control. A tragedy. But there is no alternative but to continue to trust the tyres on other vehicles because, by and large, the tyre works out as the safest mechanism for us to travel on.

Using the tyre as a metaphor, one can move very **swiftly sideways into pensions** and to take the analogy further, one can see the foundation of a transport system as a good road. It is fixed. The road is provided by the State and it is designed to have a good surface to deal with weather conditions normally associated with the local climate.

The road would compare to the Basic State Pension. It is a platform. A surface upon which everything else depends.

The thing is that most modern road surfaces would not wear well if the wheels on our cars and cycles were metal-rimmed or even if we used solid tyres. Vehicles would damage the road surface and put the cost of road maintenance up alarmingly.

TYRES ARE LIKE PENSION SCHEMES

The roads are built to accommodate pneumatic tyres. The interaction between the two surfaces is optimised to benefit both the comfort of the traveller and the responsible authority. The road surface is neither too sharp nor too dull, which gives the tyre and the vehicle that it is supporting optimal directional control.

The analogy continues with pensions because although tyres are generally considered as the same: radial, high performance, high pressure etc. the vehicle that sits on top and is supported by the wheels may vary enormously. Its weight, its size, its application etc. We, in general terms, would categorise it as more 'custom-built' than the tyre. The tyre's only perceived difference is its size and operational pressure perhaps.

Most of us are not tyre specialists.

The vehicles would be analogous to Personal Pensions and Occupational Pensions. These are strictly commercial arrangements. What you elect to have is entirely dependent upon what you consider appropriate. What you can afford.

The age at which you purchase a vehicle can determine its specification, which is parallel to considering the age at which you enter a pension contract (how far you will travel), at what age you wish to retire, (where you want to get to) and so on.

There are differing schemes; some of which allow you freedom to invest in business property (what you want to carry).

You would not buy a van if what you required was a family car. You would not buy a sports car if you had three children to transport (well, not if you had any sense anyway).

Yet the essential facility is the bit between the 'vehicle' and the 'road'. The tyre. It is what provides the cushion; that optimises the comfort, controllability, direction etc. for the majority of individuals.

The analogy with a tyre is the easiest way to explain what is going on with the Welfare State and the current move to improve pension benefits. The relationship falls in line with what Lord Beveridge would have called his 'subsistence level' National Insurance Fund.

Instead of having, as the East Germans did, everybody driving a 'Trabant', or the Russians, with everybody driving a 'Moskavitch', all the same colour, we have a choice, but with an underpin of conformity and security.

However, one might experience the 'one in a million explosive blow out' which would affect a minority of those involved, but works to the general good of the vast majority of the population in providing the very best of benefits to meet the minimum requirements. A 'smooth journey'.

There are always those with vested interest who want to introduce a 'jacked-up' suspension, balloon tyres or special type vehicles, which are purely, and simply, for racing or for show. They are not allowed on the public roads because they are inherently unsafe in that 'normal' environment.

It is not the vehicle or the road that is unsafe or unstable, it is that intermediate mechanism. In the wrong environment it is dangerous to inexperienced 'drivers'.

So it is with pensions.

SPECIFICATION IS CRUCIAL

If inferior cross-ply tyres were used on modern vehicles, we would have more explosive blow outs. They would not stand the high speeds, the temperatures and the manoeuvring that is required.

That is why organisations are promoting the current structure for a Second Tier Pension that will allow a whole variety of Occupational and Personal Pension schemes to have a firm base upon which to 'ride' and the security of knowledge that there is an earnings-related mechanism, specific to you, between the basic pension, (the road) and any other 'bodywork' you might wish to use as a 'savings' vehicle.

Why would you pay the extra money to fit special tyres if you are never going to need whatever they are going to provide? To fit 'town and country' tyres to a saloon car that is only going to drive on motorways is ludicrous. An off-road vehicle, on the other hand, would not last five minutes with low profile, low suspension, under-gear.

Basically, let those who want special tyre requirements pay the extra and get what they want.

With-profit funds have out-performed other institutionalised forms of investment on a regular basis for the last one hundred years. Their profitability is fed back to those who subscribe to appropriate schemes. Therefore, they are of mutual benefit, with Managed Funds passing part of the profitability back to the managers. The 'normal' range of tyre specifications cost far less than 'special' types do. The analogy works in this comparison.

If you are travelling on the average road, you get to your destination just as quickly as the person who cuts in and out of traffic using up more fuel, more anxiety and putting themselves and others more at risk.

That is equally true of the Second Tier Pension. Politicians would do well to listen to the average 'driver' than to pay too much heed to those with 'specialist requirements'.

Pension schemes and individual policies have proven their worth in British society. Just because there is an occasional 'explosive blow out' – like 'Maxwell' we should not lose our sense of perspective.

CHAPTER 8

PARK AND RIDE

All of our major cities seem to be getting into the 'Park and Ride' syndrome in one way or another. Oxford is held up as a national example of how the 'Park and Ride' system should work.

The Oxford Transportation System is famous – but is it for the right reasons? Oxford is in acute metaphoric 'cardiac' arrest.

Let those who commute into our cities "park up and ride in".

That is the slogan, but does it work?

Charles Handey's book 'The Age of Unreason' tells us that workforces are going to become more disparate. **People will not have desks.** There will be an 'itinerant workforce' moving 'in and out' of an office environment during the day, utilising whatever **work station** happens to be available to them at the time: then going off somewhere else to 'do their work'. A virtual office with 'live' desks.

NO HOME TO HANG YOUR HAT

Sounds a bit like our kids at school now doesn't it? No more desks or coat hangers that **you can claim as 'your own'**, merely a huge void into which you enter and from which you are eventually discharged. **An environment devoid of personal responsibility and 'comfort'.** A totally 'insecure' environment. A seat of loneliness for a territorial animal, the human being.

These hapless nomadic souls will now have to park on the outskirts of the city, and catch a bus to some preordained point. The individual will then walk with their laptop computer, client files, lunch, and whatever else they have to carry to their 'work station', if they can locate one, at their destination.

The worker will then do 'their bit' for three-quarters of an hour, two hours, whatever, then walk back to a predetermined point, hoping and praying that the vehicle that they require to board has space to allow them on. (Have you ever tried York City's 'Park and Ride' and made it on to the bus first time?)

The 'nomad' is then expected to get back to their car, go and do 'their customer based work' and then come back and commit to the process once again for the next part of the day.

Would you work in that way? Voluntarily?

York is specifically mentioned because when people <u>visit</u> York; or Oxford or Plymouth and other major cities, they will perhaps **use 'Park and Ride'.**

As **a tourist, or visitor**, one can ask the bus drivers for directions to one's destination and invariably find them very helpful.The visitor can probably cater for one or two specific calls in the locality, then find their way back to a bus (in York they are usually well used by 'shoppers') and so to the 'Park and Ride' car park, and depart.

The tariff is very reasonable. **The visitor's schedule is broadly predictable**. But would you commit to the process daily, as a commuter, in your own environment?

WHO IS 'A SHOPPER'?

Some basic experiments **concluded that between 60-70% of an inner city's trade and commerce was conducted by commuters**, people who actually work in the city or town, each day. Small 'white good' or 'gift' items can be fairly heavy to carry or fragile in nature and, therefore, **having 'the car' handy is very useful**. The prime shopping time in a city mid-week is between 11.30am and 3.00pm. That is the time when part-time workers begin and end their 'shift'. It covers lunch breaks.

Specific 'shopping' areas were identified. The figures were verified in research conducted by the British Retail Association. It was concluded that 'out of town' shopping malls thrive in the early morning, seven till ten, and late afternoon, early evening; as commuters move to and from their place of work and commit themselves to a shopping 'experience'.

The 'greys' are entertainment shoppers. The retired community shops for recreation: not buying, shopping.

Endeavours to find local authorities that have conducted this sort of research conclude that very few, if any, have. Therefore, the local authority's complete car parking and 'Park and Ride' strategy **is based upon a perception**.

The City Engineering Department and councillors' perception is **"keep the commuters out so that there is more space for shoppers to park."** The relationship between the commuters and shoppers has been totally lost on the 'politicians'. Yet those politicians are the greatest proponents for closing car parks down or **shortening the duration of stay to one or two hours; to "facilitate shoppers"**.

But is it to 'facilitate' or are the authorities merely inducing turnover of cars to increase the revenue to the local authority's coffers?

Tourists wishing to spend the day in a locality are similarly discouraged from spending time, as well as their money, in the central environment. Who can relax and enjoy a visit to an area if it is curtailed, by bureaucracy, to a few hours?

Traffic issues are so sensitive to individuals locally; particularly when **you** are a motorist who wants to use **your car** battling against **a politician who uses a bike** to attend his council meetings.

ENVIRONMENTAL EGOTISM

But shouldn't the environmentalists have their way?

Yes: provided they **have facts** to back up their hypotheses. Global warming has been shown to be a natural phenomenon due to the 'living' nature of our planet. Factual evidence that 'mankind' has contributed to the phenomenon is as sparse as that for the 'millennium bug' switching all our power off.

Motorcar engines have, over the past ten years, improved to such an extent that they now produce 15% or less of the emissions that they did ten years ago. Heavy goods vehicles and particularly public service vehicles have experienced no such magnitude of improvement - **of course they are working on it. It takes time, effort, money...and incentive.**

Devon County Council have used a very novel mechanism to ensure that the public service vehicles that perform their school runs on contract are always at the **leading edge of environmental advancement**. Tenders are sought, but no vehicle over five years old is allowed to fulfil that tender contract.

The County Council pays slightly more for the service than do other councils but their environment is maintained at the 'technological thresholds' at all times. Older buses are sold to the less ingenious and progressive areas of the country to provide their cheap and cheerless 'Park and Ride' systems or school bus service runs. There is little margin for profit to buy new vehicles when forced to operate at 'penny-pinching' rates.

Oxford's contamination and congestion causes shoppers to avoid the city centre. Good city centre parking for clean 'environmentally friendly' cars would solve much of the problem.

The Chambers of Commerce are very supportive of **'Park and Ride'** systems **provided that they can be commercially viable**. Politicians may be failing to accept that the 'environmental problem' has moved on.

Would examination of the facts confirm that people would use public transport, if available? Consider existing facilities and suitable 'Park and Ride' locations.

TESTING THE PARK AND RIDE THEORY

One of the busiest routes into a city passes a small town, which has **a railway station and a bus service.**

There are probably 4000 people living in the town, many of whom will work in the nearby City, which is a mere seven miles away. **The railway journey is less than 15 minutes and the return fare £2.20.** Five days a week is £11 and you could probably get an annual ticket. The cost of car parking is higher than the fare at £3.60 per day. A great incentive, which is widely taken up?

Assume that 10% of the population of the town work in the city: 400 people. They would be fairly regular in their habits. But let's say only half of them were city-based workers: 200 people.

There are plenty of trains that provide for normal office hours.

The 'town' is quite well endowed with individual car parking spaces that attach to the houses of the commuters. They are extremely secure and are within a few minutes walk of the station.

Between **six and twelve people per day board the train** to go to the city in the morning. **Much the same number come back at night.** If 'Park and Ride' was going to be a success for commuters; as politicians would have us believe, **do you think that it would be reasonable that more people would use this particular facility?**

If you perceived that there was something wrong with the facility that detracted from people using it what action would you take, as a local politician?

a)   Would you ask people in the city centre who have no knowledge of the town or its environment, what they would do?

b)   Would you perhaps conduct a house-to-house enquiry in the town to establish what could be done to improve the facility?

c)   Would you contact the provider of the facility and ask them why no-one is using the excellent service that they are providing?

d)   Would you take some other form of action, and what would it be?

Did the local council or the County Council do any of those things?

The answer is no.

IT'S A VISITOR THING

They concluded that they had better **lay some other service on from somewhere remote** and **spend hundreds of thousands of pounds building an out-of-town car park** in an **endeavour to prove** that **Park and Ride really could work.**   Instead of trains, of course, **they would use buses.** That, in their view, **would solve the problem.**

Interestingly enough, **two local County Council engineers** were asked why they did not use the railway. They observed that there was really no need because "they did not find themselves looking down someone else's exhaust pipe before reaching the sanctuary of the County Council car park; **driving was far more convenient.**"

Another statistic, which is quoted by the City Council, is; "why should the 38% of residents who do not own cars have to provide facilities for those who do?"

The fact that there are the young, old, infirm or just plain non-drivers seems to be lost on the Council. Many people live in the City because they have local transport or can walk back and forth to work and can be wonderfully environmentally friendly.

The car parks raise millions of pounds per year in revenues that support those without personal transport and provide them with facilities.

CHAPTER 9

MEDIA HYPE – AN OVERREACTIVE FORCE

As we all follow that plaintive cry from a distant corner of the shopping mall or outside the tube station, against the bus stop: "ennin' Stanarr", we seek to quench our inexorable thirst for news.

News! It is more akin to the Eric Morcombe sketch, as Ernie Wise tries to 'put the newspaper seller right' on the pronunciation of 'Evening Standard'; only to find that the tabloid newspaper that he purchases is indeed **a corruption not only of the English language, but of the truth**.

The politicians, in true '*Yes Prime Minister*' style, cover every crisis with overreaction and what they see as public favour, when detailed research and cool appraisal would be a more productive mechanism. The media lends a 'helping hand' at every opportunity.

The baying hounds that we hear are not those of the fox hunt tracking down some hapless 'Reynard', they are more like the cheeping trills of **'Chicken Licken' screaming, in innocence of the facts** and with misguided knowledge, that "the sky is falling," gathering an ever greater entourage around him as 'Clucky Lucky' and all the rest of the menagerie build up momentum only to be eaten by the fox, or, once hunger has been sated, to be destroyed anyway and left to rot.

TV PRODUCER SPONSORED

A nation in crisis? Or a world in crisis? It depends upon how the editor or programme producer 'sees' it.

What we encounter is a manifestation of media hype and political intrigue that has probably been a facet of the human race for its entire existence but is now amplified to crescendo level by the **instantaneous response** of clicking cameras and satellite transmitted television pictures that bring chaos and

65

carnage, worry and, occasionally, hope, into our businesses and homes at the flick of a switch.

The news is there almost before it has happened. And why can we not ignore it? Well, first of all we are nosy, and secondly humans appear to have an insatiable appetite to perpetuate worry, even if it is someone else's problem. That is why I am writing this. Bizarre or what?

Worry is an Anglo-Saxon word meaning strangulation. Surely the message from 'Chicken Licken' that we teach to our young children is; **don't react until you have found out what the facts are.**

WHAT MAKES YOU THINK THAT?

It was an acorn, not the sky, that had fallen. 'Chicken Licken' needed to find out where 'the King' (authority) was before rushing off in every direction to find him. If it <u>was</u> the sky that was falling; could anyone do anything about it?

Well, seemingly the "Greens" can. It is not to say that improvements cannot be made to our environmental condition. Of course. But once those improvements have been made (cars now emit 15% of the toxins that they threw out ten years ago) one has to **acknowledge that those things have been done.**

Achievement is, after all, achievement. Achievement, apparently, is seldom 'news'.

Utopia has yet to be discovered. If you took every motor vehicle off the road, and everyone got on bikes, the impact on our environment would be minuscule, except that is in the medical world where **hospital admissions would rise** due to accidents, and the practical world where everything would regress.

The accident and personal injury rate was far higher when bikes roamed the earth. China and the Asian subcontinent still reflect the horrendously high levels of death and disfigurement due to cycling accidents. Horse-drawn

66

vehicles were dangerous in physical terms. The overproduction of manure ("hoss muck" if you are a Northerner) was such that it became a hazard to health in its own right, a very unpleasant form of aroma therapy.

Seemingly the research into those facts is not as intriguing to universities as such hugely important topics as:

'do we get wetter in the rain if we run or walk?'

Or, of course, that more modern topic of intrigue:

'do penguins really fall over backwards when an aeroplane flies over them (or is it just a myth that the military have dreamt up for their own amusement?)'

Let's spend a couple of million pounds to find out!

"Does it really matter?"

CHILD'S NIGHT OUT

Politicians and the 'newshounds' have treated us like children. One has to say that there is a proportion of society that has reacted in that childlike manner, but does that mean that none of us have any intelligence apart from those who seek to guide us?

Edwina (no more curried eggs for me) Currie, has a lot to answer for in respect of the destruction of a large part of the poultry industry, which has never recovered from her Department's interference.

You remember the old adage "go to work on an egg," well, of course, eggs became bad for us because of high cholesterol. Coupled with Curry's misconceptions on salmonella the egg industry actually had a 'double whammy' to contend with.

Salmonella and heart conditions led to the advice **"do not eat more than one egg per week because of the health hazard."**

67

Salmonella turned out, in very simplistic terms, to be a problem with bringing our chicks up in a 'poo-free' environment instead of letting them peck droppings as their natural instincts told them to.

One night in the House of Lords there was a major debate. Their lordships ate egg mayonnaise with their evening meals. All was well until the next day when twenty-seven of their lordships suffered from that 'is he still in there?' syndrome that we spoke of earlier.

"Oh... I never use that foreign mayonnaise stuff. I always use salad cream."

"Mmmmmmmm, I know what you mean, you really can't trust this foreign food can you?"

But of course the Les Dawson sketch on that basis would have been far removed from the truth. It was English eggs that had salmonella in them.

Edwina Currie, the then **Minister for Agriculture, acted immediately**. No, she did not fire the chef at the House of Commons, nor did she offer to pay their lordships' laundry bill. She sent **80 million chickens to the gallows** and put thousands of small business poultry breeders, layers and processing units out of business.

Of course, **the problem was hygiene**. Not the chef's hygiene; the chicken's hygiene. Well, **more directly the chick's hygiene**.

CHICKEN S**T

As Ken was explaining to Bill:

> "It is quite simple you see, when the chicks hatch in the natural environment, they scratches about in the soil and they peck at the older birds' droppings."

In fact this is, apparently, quite normal for all fowl. Watch your budgerigar.

Bill questioned what Ken was getting at.

"Well," he went on to explain. "It is quite simple really, mass-produced chicks, or more specifically laying hens eggs, are hatched in an incubator, so the chick has just its own hygienic environment of straw and stuff, the feeder and some water surrounding it. It never pecks the droppings of other birds, there are none.

"A bit of grit," I think that is what he said, "never hurt anybody, because in the droppings are bacteria which go into the chick's stomach and develop within it into adulthood. Those bacteria kill off the salmonella bacteria, thus keeping the problem down to a minimum. Most of the bacteria in any animal's gut is essential and beneficial."

Well, that may be an old farmer's tale but there are a lot of people who now spray their chicken houses with 'guano' for the chicks to peck at.

Of course, the 'politically correct' method is to inject all the poultry with antibiotics so that not only are the salmonella bacteria killed, the drugs kill everything else as well.

"And let's face it," Ken said, "if you cook the food properly, then salmonella is not a problem."

But of course **that answer is far too cheap and has no commercial interest to anybody.**

Chicken s**t comes free.

The byproduct of the whole "egg catastrophe" is that power devolved to the larger producers an unnecessary imposition of slaughter, destruction and regulation, brought about by Government and media hype, took its toll on those less able to withstand its rigours.

Ah! but was that an isolated case?

BULL S**T

What about BSE and beef? What about it?

Millions, or is it billions, of pounds of public money has been spent on a fruitless cause. Sixteen volumes of telephone directory size material has been produced, only to conclude what many instinctively knew right from the start. **BSE was a load of bull**.

Million of pounds could have been spent on leukaemia research benefiting hundreds of thousands of young lives per year – Alzheimer's disease, a dreadful cost to society; or heart research. But no, a huge sum of money was spent because ten people were diagnosed with CJD over a five-year period.

The interesting thing about the BSE crisis is **that none of the reports in the press or the public domain go back to what farmers who reared the beast talk about most.** A world shortage of oil.

The last fuel crisis, 1972/74, brought about not only the spectacular collapse of the stock market as the index dropped from 1500 down to 147, but also **a huge rise in oil prices**, which our "friends" in the European Union got very concerned about.

In an **endeavour to save fuel**, a directive was made that the cooking temperature of protein-reinforced animal feeds should be **reduced** from **400°C to 270°C**. There doesn't seem to be any mention of that fact in the 16 volumes, nor in the one and a half inch thick tome that was produced **by MAFF on the subject in 1998**, but the temperature reduction and 'cooking' method change does seem to have been an arbitrary, **unresearched decision**.

It does seem rather a basic thing that you should not feed ruminants or herbivores, pretty well strictly vegetarian beasts in other words, on carnivorous products. Ordinary men and women instinctively know that there is something wrong with that practice. But, **have the people who made the decision paid the price?** The **civil servants have been promoted or moved** to an alternative department.

HORSE S**T

Once again it is the large abattoirs, the large producers that will have survived and those least able in society to sustain themselves, **those with the greatest love of their animals that they had to slaughter**, those with families and homes to lose; they have become the waste discarded by that sly old fox that everyone wants to protect.

The politician, the civil servant, the local official, the media hack, who, in their quest to satisfy their aspirations are not content with enough for their own appetite but get caught up in the metaphor that is "overkill". And the **newshound is in there baying for blood** and goading the sceptical on to even greater excesses.

Surely **'leadership' is the quest** of the political brain and the desire of the public employee?

But **no, it is control.** It is control that drives them to such noticeable misdirection.

Ever since the railways were denationalised every excuse for a front-page story has led to a call for the re-formation of British Rail. Whether that is right or wrong, the re-formation of British Rail is a matter for fact not of hypothesis. However, it does seem that rail travel is still one of **the safest and surest forms of travel**, statistically, whether publicly or privately owned.

In all of the 'horrific accidents', the survivors who walked away from the "carnage" outnumber those who unfortunately died or were severely maimed. The number of carriages left standing square and upright seem to outnumber those that were disfigured and toppled.

Where were the headlines proclaiming safety, security? In comparison to a coach crash at 110 miles an hour we should have been delighted with the outcome for so many travellers, yet every effort was made to **besmirch the engineers "responsible" for the broken rail,** or to cover up the responsibility of an errant driver.

An almost instant **£15 billion** was made available and the railway system sent into reverse whilst "urgent" engineering work is undertaken.

The **same regulator** that formulated the political give-away **is responsible for much of the sluggishness** of the system **by imposing fines on rail operators** that merely **delay trains to give their travelling customers a better service** by ensuring that a **connecting service** is made.

The overriding authority of the rail regulator appears to have been to take **precious capital resources away** from the workface by way of fines, a disincentive to an efficient service, which fails miserably to compete adequately with the fat controller. Thomas and his friends at least recognised the **fallibility of the system from time to time** and the need for flexibility. Even a humble vicar understood the vagaries of the system.

Just as BSE and CJD are seemingly unrelated. Just as the millions and millions of pounds that have been poured into the health service for AIDS is totally out of proportion to the requirements of a society which is dying of cancer, heart disease and other much more deserving yet less public considerations, so rail mismanagement, pensions mis-selling and endowment mortgages also **transpire to be figments of fertile imagination and dubious mathematics.**

If only politicians had brains the rest of us would lack the intelligence to be concerned at their actions, **but the general population**, which sought to employ or elect professional people, with an objective view, to look after the greater administration of not only the nation but local areas of responsibility too, **are being poorly served.**

MEDIA 'LEADERS'

Journalists have been feeding as damaging a concoction to the public as any farmyard cow. They are now **exhibiting the same disoriented symptoms** of their bovine cousins with BSE.

Our children are brought up in such a sterile environment that they, like the chicks, fail to follow Granny's premise of "eating a peck of dirt before you die".

Of course one in a hundred thousand will get something nasty, but surely that is life. Life is for living. We have to take risks, which is why the pensions mis-selling nausea is so corrupt.

The myth is perpetuated by a media whose ignorance is only surpassed by its arrogance. People make decisions and continue to make them, and a decision made surely has to be carried through. They are your decisions. They are therefore your responsibility.

Regulation is merely an expression of the overbearing mechanism for pricing people out of existence through control.

If only politicians had the brains to use common sense instead of consultants, write their own speeches instead of talking other people's words, research problems thoroughly with an unbiased, objective view, what a really objective overview of real issues there would be. **They could even constrain the freedom of the press by the principle of subjudice – don't shout until the trial or enquiry is complete.**

Then we could all lift our heads from looking at the pavement to avoid walking in the 'poo'.

If you walk with your head high you will not notice it when you do step in it, and your nose will be far enough away from it to avoid the smell.

A consultant is someone who seldom has the balls to run their own business, but has the gall to tell others how to run theirs.

CHAPTER 10

SELECTIVE REPORTING

We have a great tradition in Western society of following our noses, and when it comes to saving for the future, our noses can sometimes lead us into places we would rather not be.

Well, 'rather not be' is probably the wrong expression. You see: **we don't know what we don't know**. So when we are told things that contradict what we don't know, then we don't know that what we are being told is not quite right. You didn't know that did you?

One can almost imagine the Spaniards descending upon the Incas and saying,

> "Oh you really do not want all of that gold stuff that you keep digging out of the ground, but we have got a use for it, have a case of our best red wine instead.
>
> It will make you feel good for a day, you will have a headache when you wake up tomorrow but it is great stuff and it is a lot better than that gold rock you keep melting down and making trinkets out of."

Of course they would have said it in Spanish; but, if it were quoted here in Spanish few readers would have understood the point being made!

Or it may be that one could visualise the explorers and developers of Africa: the forebears of a famous diamond 'house', convincing the local populace that they should give up their land and mineral rights for a case of their best pilsner. Well, it's a Dutch thing. And at least you do not get those terrible headaches from drinking it – it just makes you fall about and vomit.

GOOD FOR THE GOOSE

So it is with financial services. Newspaper financial columnists who have to fill something between 36 to 64 pages of financial nausea every week create their own stories. It makes good copy and it sells newspapers, but does it help the public?

How about this for a story then, **you tell those who 'don't know'** (the equivalent of the Incas and the African tribesmen) that their **endowments will not pay off their mortgages**. The informants do not exactly say that **endowments** are **useless** but they do state that the value may not be as much as it was thought it might be.   Could that be because life assurance companies do not bother advertising in their newspapers any more? Well, possibly.

The journalists then seek to **convince those who have money** that they should **buy 'secondhand endowments'** (seemingly because they are worthless and will not produce as much as people thought).

To summarise: **those with scant financial resources** are persuaded by journalists to **sell their 'poor value' chance** of making some real financial gain to **those who can afford to speculate**, but would rather not, because the chance of the 'poor value' savings plan being **'good value' is better than average**.

Those purveying secondhand endowments do advertise in the papers. There is no correlation surely?

Who could possibly explain to the 'don't know' individuals that if they stop paying into their savings plan at year five, all of the **costs**, which had previously been spread forward over the next twenty years, would now **have to be recovered**. Contrast that to year twenty when there would only be five years to go: an early 'cash in' value of the policy could then register anything up to 12-13% return on each contribution paid. That is the average return in the millennium year.

It is no wonder that the poor old Incas and the African tribesmen were puzzled is it? But then they eventually realised that they were being cheated by the informants and went to war!

ENDOWMENTS AND MORTGAGES

What looks good as a short-term remedy hides an exponential return for the future. Exponential is a big word for saying that the rate of return gets higher and higher as the endowment progresses through the years. Not as a straight line but as an upward bending curve.

	Years	£ Repayment	£ Cash Value Low Cost Endowment	£ Cumulative Endowment Premiums
Capital repaid OR Repayable from LCEAWP £50,000 mortgage @ 7.71% - 24 nb. Non smoker	7	5,808	7,164	7,824
	15	18,055	31,111	16,765
	20	30,084	59,109	22,353
	25	50,000	163,054	27,942
Total interest paid at 25 years		56,977	96,375	
Total cost of house purchase including Life Insurance. LCEAWP £93.14/mth. TI £15.50		111,627	124,317	
Capital repaid		50,000	50,000	
Possible Cash in Hand		Nil	113,054	
Possible excess over costs available		Nil	38,737	

LCEAWP = Low Cost Endowment Assurance With profits   TI = Term Insurance

A mortgage table shows how much you would pay off of your mortgage debt in a capital repayment mortgage at specific points on a mortgage cycle.

The interesting thing to note is that by the time a point **twenty years** out of the **twenty-five year cycle** on **a repayment mortgage** is reached, **only half of the capital has been repaid**. The last half has got to be paid in the last five years.

An endowment policy works on a very similar basis, the last five years on a twenty-five year policy will see the amount payable to the policy holder double, historically. Historically **the cash-in value at twenty years** of a twenty-five year term **would pay off all of the mortgage!**

Put simply; this means that **"the don't know that they don't know, people"** sell their policies at a point where they have paid a large proportion of the costs, and hand that policy over to **somebody else who is going to reap the benefits** of 'the don't knows' generosity (or ignorance). Silly isn't it?

It is the sort of thing that you see in all of the *Crocodile Dundee* **films**. The bad guy is trying to **use the native ignorance to steal the gold or the icon** or whatever it is. *Crocodile Dundee* sweeps in to make it all right again. What a very nice chap he is, a sort of latter day Tarzan I guess.

So who is your latter day Tarzan?

Well, it does not appear to be the Financial Services Authority because they seem to be on the side of the gunrunners.

WHEN LITTLE IS BIG

Just imagine that historically a **twenty-five year endowment** with £100 per month being paid into it **matured at £202,000.** That is about middle market for what has been achieved on that generic style of contract in the year 2000. The policy would have been taken out in 1975 when inflation was rushing towards 25%.

ARE THE CURRENT ENDOWMENT INVESTMENT PROJECTIONS REALISTIC?

The Government has supported a misinformation campaign by the Financial Services Regulator that reduces a

£202,000
maturity
to a
£56,000
forecast

Those who regulate what assurance companies can indicate to the public **insist** that the assuror can only **project a return of £56,000 instead of the £202,000** actually being paid.

It is by that mechanism, telling those who "don't know that they don't know" that their policies are going to mature at just over a quarter of what they are actually maturing at, **that they, inadvertently perhaps, persuade ordinary people to sell their endowments to those far more able to make money** out of the **others' misguided misfortune**, that the real damage is done.

And those nice **men and women who write for the newspapers**, well you would be lucky to find one of them technically qualified, and most of them might just as well write in Spanish, but like the Spanish Conquistador in South America, they will **do what they do "for the good of the people"**. Even if the people cannot understand the full implications of their utterances.

We all know which people they are doing it for the good of. And it is not you.

But what have the bureaucrats got to gain?

MAKING WORK!

Well, it could not be high salaries or non-contributory pensions could it?

We are told that the authorities have to **pay 'over the top wages'** and have to give 'non-contributory pension rights', along with other perks, because otherwise **people would not seek to be employed**. But they are honourable people.

There is always a market place for somebody to work for the regulator isn't there?

Go back in time to Prince John and the history books will illustrate the point. That is until 'they' rewrite the history books of course.

It must be tough hiring people to burn people's eyes out, chop off the odd limb, or have a little hanging party. Mustn't it? I mean; you would not do it for the pure fun of it, would you?

It is a bit like Hitler and Milosevic; and probably Stalin, together with some of our recent African leaders: **you have to pay people enough for it to be an incentive to do dastardly things.** But once you have got them in your employ, by God, you have got them. That is the great thing; there is no way out. The public, those that are regulated, have to realise the plot before you become 'persona non grata', therefore the trick is to stay ahead of the game. In that position of course you would use any mechanism at your disposal to protect your own position and make sure you were never exposed. That might **lead to public misinformation, propaganda, creative thinking, all those things that end up like 'pension mis-selling', the endowment 'problems', denigrating the motor industry (losing £2 million a day and 'profiteering' whilst it is doing so) and so on.**

If you had fields and fields full of tens of thousands of surplus cars that you had produced, wouldn't you reduce the price to get rid of them? You may even hope that you would appease your detractors, like the Consumer Association, and **pray that you survived to come back another day** and actually make a profit.

Chrysler may have come back from 'the dead' all those years ago, but there are many motor industry manufacturers who did not last the course. And those that do survive the current situation will reap a very dubious benefit.

What of the situation where the patient goes to see a physician and the doctor tells her that she is terminally ill, and then proceeds to poison the chalice that she is drinking her medicine from?

We are told that the life assurance industry is terminally ill, and also the motor industry, but just like Doctor Shipman, who now languishes in gaol for his efforts, **perhaps we should check who is giving the diagnosis and whether they are to be the beneficiary** when the so called 'terminally ill' patient dies.

CHAPTER 11

A GREAT NATION UNDERMINED

We are a great nation and, of course, our media often tell us so.

When our national football team beat the German national team for the first time since 1966 in the Euro 2000 competition, the Daily Telegraph heralded the event with an outsize photograph, centre front page, of a miscreant youth **using a plastic chair to smash up the front of a café.**

'Our shame', as their headline put it, is not in the youth but in the fact **that he got so much publicity for what was a side-show to the main event.** Perhaps if they did not get the publicity they would not enter into the activity. And even if they did, so what, let the police deal with it and let the court case be dealt with in the inside pages.

"IT'S GOOD NEWS WEEK"

The front page for once surely could, and should, have heralded the good news about what is, after all, our national sport. **WE WON.**

But no, the media chose to feed us the information that they want to feed us, and denigrate whatever good there seems to be in society. There is a lot of generous inherent 'goodness' in our society.

So it is with volunteerism. **Gordon Brown** reportedly declared that volunteers should be **"paid to encourage them to volunteer"**. Perhaps he should examine the facts. But then the media would not help him there either.

Many of you will have seen the series '*Airport*' and taken in the vast array of circumstances that are created in that microcosm of society.

Well, imagine if you will, **thirty young adults** between eighteen and twenty-six years of age on their way to Central America as volunteers. They were **setting out to rebuild a bridge**, which is a vital link between a village and a main township in Haiti.

The leader, a committed Christian, had assembled the group. They had raised their own funds to enable them to buy provisions and provide shelter for their expedition. They had not made a fuss about going. **They were going in humility** to do some good work and then return to their normal occupations or studies once the job had been completed.

However, when a three-man camera team rushed into the airport terminal anxiously looking for their 'quarry', the team leader felt a tinge of pride.

Somebody had obviously notified the media about his eighteen youngsters and the 'good work' that they were about to do. Of course, he soon became crestfallen.

What a silly man to even think that the media would turn out, outside of office hours too, to deal with his insignificant contribution to society.

No, they had come for something far more important - **the return of three thugs from Holland** who once again made the media's front pages for the fight that they had caused at a football match.

Contrast that with an anecdotal report of scenes from a hotel window when a major German football team was in competition against a major Dutch team. The hotel was in Amsterdam and chaos reigned outside as conflicting supporters of these two great teams confronted each other, overturned cars, set fire to a fire engine and so on.

There were no cameras, no arc lights, no intrusive media and, what is more important, in **the next day's morning papers, there was no mention of the mischief, just the event.**

The headline ran **'Ajax beat Bayern Munich.'**

A focus on the good can leave a better taste in the mouth and again let the inside pages deal with the bad for the benefit of those who want to know about these things. And we should all want to know about these things, but in the correct perspective.

WORTH TEN PRESSED MEN

Volunteerism is an interesting concept that is manifestly misunderstood by some politicians, most of whom, one assumes, were volunteers at some stage in their political careers.

Volunteerism is difficult to put into perspective but if 'Mr Arkwright' at 'Arkwright's corner shop' always trusted his delivery boy to run the shop whilst he, Mr Arkwright, took time out from the shop during opening hours (and or course the shop is "open all hours") then Mr Arkwright would lose personal revenue.

The alternative way of looking at the situation, of course, is that the 'Mr Arkwrights' of the world are using their personal revenue to do good works. They spend part of that personal revenue on putting staff in the shop to do the 'trade' work required during the proprietor's absence.

'Mr Arkwright', for example, has no time for courting with 'Nurse Gladys' because he cannot spare time away from his shop – unless he employs staff. **Any time away from the shop detracts from earning a living.**

Contrast that situation with a position that prevails in a number of local authorities, where time is allowed for individuals to stand as local councillors in any other council area than that of the authority that employed them.

Hundreds, if not thousands, of employees of local authorities are able to gain positions on the policy-making core of any authority 'where they do not work'.

This facility enables individuals to take trades union posts and/or local authority posts as councillors in 'other' authorities. The individuals are allowed to take time off, with expenses paid, by the organisation that they were doing "voluntary" work for, whilst also being paid a full salary and 'clocking up' an earnings-related pension paid for by the public.

The local authority could be receiving less than 50 or 60% value from the employment contract that they have with that individual. **The public are paying for 'political' volunteerism, without knowing it.**

HOME FROM HOME WITH DISABILITIES

Following the Second World War, Sir Leonard Cheshire devoted his time and resources to founding and establishing a network of what became known as the Cheshire Homes. These homes are run as **charitable institutions for the disabled** on the basis of a purely charitable foundation. Sue Ryder Homes work on much the same basis. Yet they are under threat from Government as are those that provide similar services.

A privately run residential home providing excellent accommodation, which those who live in the homes respect and enjoy due to the care of specialist staff, is being **emasculated by bureaucracy.**

The facilities, providing staff who wash, dress, feed and assist their residents with various disabilities under one roof, have got to close. "They" have determined that it is better that those **people currently receiving care are returned to the community**. Returned to the community and what kind of future?

Returning to 'Arkwright' and 'Nurse Gladys'. Both of those individuals in their own way perform a local social service, **but many similar facilities have already ceased to exist in local communities.**

'Arkwright' knows all of the gossip, but most importantly knows all the people involved in the gossip. 'Nurse Gladys' is a district nurse performing a difficult function in a close community.

Nursing homes make up a microcosm of that same social involvement. Knowledge of people, recognition of personal distress and the provision of a helping hand, cost effectively, on a local basis, without too much difficulty, is their hallmark.

Placing the **disabled into the community** whilst they are still physically or mentally unable to cope in that community merely creates a greater strain on the hundreds of real 'Nurse Gladyses' in the country and **removes the individual's security** of swift response.

Unfortunately 'Arkwright style' corner shops have disappeared in a world beset with the love of **'control'**. That is what the large supermarkets exert and what Government finds appealing.

In short, **what politicians achieve is not a return to the community but a condemnation to isolation and frustration.** Often family units are disparate groupings where children leave home early to settle in other areas.

VOLUNTEERISM VERSUS EXTORTIONISM

Those who care so much provide genuine charity in society; they devote their personal time, energy and expertise to those who need their help.

Of course sometimes they fail because of financial constraints. That is part of life. Life entails risk. The bureaucratic machine also fails, and those who suffer as a result have little more, if any, redress.

Surely Government would be better supporting volunteerism and 'charitable' enterprises. Funds are withdrawn with little notice as political agendas affected by outside influences change.

The fact is, however, that **the Treasury now extracts £3.2 billion from charities** through 'back door' taxation to 'fund' its malignant social programme's growth **every year**. The removal of tax credits on equity investments is squalid extortion.

The power of the television media in particular is against society's best interests on many occasions.

The local authority because of a BBC film documentary closed down a privately funded residential home. Police were called in because of the nature of the 'exposé' accusations. **Yet on examining the evidence the police found that 'editorial licence' had created a great TV spectacular** that every 'nosy' television viewer feeds on, and a great story for the newspapers to carry, but **all without foundation**.

The 'fifty-five' residents of the home were thrown into turmoil as "placements" in the community were found for them. Of course the **owner** of the business, and property, **suffered an irreparable and irreversible haemorrhage of their personal finance** and, more importantly, their individual integrity.

The perpetrators of the 'real' injustice merely apologise in 'small print' whilst the public gloat as another "wrong 'un" is brought to book and 'made to pay'.

All the politicians, both local and national, would have **done better to examine the evidence and take professional advice**. Surely they had a responsibility to do what the police did, and seek to see the full BBC transcript and evidence, before they reacted in the way that they did?

"Smoke without fire" comes to mind: but it is about time we learnt that a good story currently overrides any form of moral duty and any requirement to examine facts, before "jumping the gun" and entering the 'egg on face' brigade. Those with an interest in their own success sometimes light fires in areas where, without proper control, they destroy acres of good metaphorical forest.

These incursions into insanity are inspired to give credibility to a political agenda that many would say would otherwise wither through lack of necessity.

As a journalist recently said "**we have to provide entertainment and that means headlines that draw, and contents that enthral**" – how sad. Even sadder that politicians believe the myths and act so hastily and positively upon them.

86

For all its flaws; the society held together and nurtured, for an extra penny on a packet of tea or a gallon of petrol in 'Nurse Gladys's' car, make the 'Arkwright' character of TV fiction, and real values of community, a far better barometer of what is most beneficial to life.

The dimension of "giving" being good for the soul is reflected in all major religions internationally. That aspect of volunteerism is completely disregarded by comments such as that reported in recent times as being made by Gordon Brown MP, to the effect that **those involved in charitable work should be paid for the work that they do**.

It is almost a contradiction in terms. The statement certainly illustrates a total lack of understanding of the ethos of giving, and the requirement of human beings to 'give back' to society freely in whatever enterprise they happen to be engaged in.

TAKING THE 'NICK'

Taking another Ronnie Barker caricature of life, we might view the intricacies and intimacies of prison life in a light-hearted way. Be assured that prison is far from a pleasant experience, even to visit.

Those in authority now see fit to release those who have transgressed against mankind **'back into the community'** to 'rehabilitate them'. **Politicians** hastily reassure the public that they are keeping a **'watchful eye'** on those who return.

The public may have a slightly different perception of that process, as has recently been seen from the misunderstanding of the word 'paedophile' and 'paediatric'. Enraged members of the public responding to a newspaper article drove a paediatrician from her home. **The *News of the World* justified its 'Name and Shame' exposé with great gusto.**

"Ignore the damage done, it is for the greater good."

Of course the felons are all supervised by salaried staff on earnings-related pensions whilst held at Her Majesty's pleasure, but if that 'salaried staff' fails the individuals, or through over-riding 'PC' cannot hold the situation in check, the problem falls back on a whole raft of post-incarceration charities that pick up the pieces with volunteers.

The exuberance with which **society allows the use of television** programmes **to instruct our youngsters** how to steal cars, joyride, terrorise a neighbourhood and generally learn the finer arts of the baser instincts of mankind, defies logic. **There is no escape save isolation it seems.**

Bad manners, bad language and bad practices are all handed down 'en masse' to an ever absorbent audience of fertile minds.

CHARITY BEGINS AT HOME

Over **one-third** of the adult population, and indeed a great proportion of our younger generation, are **engaged actively in benevolent or charitable works.** Britain is probably one of the most charitable communities in the world. It has always been thus. The good in people has been recognised rather than the bad. It is **what has made us a great nation**. It is **a Christian ethic**, and a legacy of our upbringing.

We have exported that charity, in huge quantities. From parish councils through to national political parties: service organisations such as Rotary, Lions and Round Table, through the Women's Institute, League of Christian Mothers to the more specific societies that look after dyslexics, children suffering from arthritis, leukaemia, cancer and heart foundations and so on. There are **great armies of people** who devote their time willingly and often at great **personal sacrifice**.

Yet there are those who still wish to impose regulation, 'order' they call it, and prescription. For the past fifteen years we have been **taught to complain more than praise**, to 'recognise' the unacceptable as 'normal behaviour', and more importantly to accept little personal responsibility for the decisions that we make as individuals concerning what we buy, the services we choose and so on.

What is clearly needed is balance. A balance to harness the innate goodness in people would be a gift indeed. People should be **encouraged to give**, and be recognised for giving, with humility, which is the way that they would wish it. We should acknowledge that individuals in society, by and large, do not do good deeds to receive something in return. They do 'good' **because they want to**. Some: because they need to.

Of course, the cynic would argue that these people are merely the pawns and puppets of those who would take advantage of them. Tell that to the **lifeboat men, volunteer firemen, those who stand on charity stalls week after week and run tombolas** for the local church. It seems to have more to do with love, charity and concern than self-interest, vanity and commercial gain. **Mr Brown should look again.**

BESET WITH FOOLS

We must not confuse regulation with dictation. We have more rules that govern our everyday life than we could ever hope to come to grips with, and yet we are held responsible if we do not act on them verbatim. We have to acknowledge that society needs rules, but those rules need to be malleable in the sense that they must be practical.

Where damage is done to another human being, either physically, mentally or financially, then of course remedies should be available, but it should be within the bounds of common sense and the ability to perform.

Those who set the rules should have perfect knowledge over what they are setting rules about. It is surely for fools to pass regulation and legislation that serves only to confuse. Such action works to the detriment of the majority in society.

We often hear the term 'dinosaurs' mentioned in the context - 'these people are like dinosaurs, they just do not adapt.'

Dinosaurs did not fail to adapt. They were not given time. An asteroid collision with earth. Dust cloud. Freezing conditions in a short period of time. Finish. Dead.

So it is with Financial Services regulation. Evolution, rather than revolution, would have allowed the dinosaur to become something different, as other animal species have, over time.

SHORT-TERM PASSION

Our politicians are inclined to 'revolution' with their annual budgets instead of a businessman's five to ten year plan. The huge bureaucracy that supports politicians is self-feeding. Control freaks eager to remain on the payroll and impress their sponsors.

It has taken tens of years to create the social intercourse and understanding that is not only apparent to those who use it, but also fundamental to the success of the 'Home Service Insurance Man'. It is gone forever.

The value for money, pound for pound invested, is certainly less sparkling than policies paid by direct debits through banks. However, **a third of the population do not have bank accounts**. The average premium size for Industrial Branch policies was measured in single unit pounds.

The current Government has **a passion for providing welfare to the poor.** It seems extraordinary that they are allowing the very core of social welfare provided through regular visits to the home, concern for the family and provision in abundance of peripheral social service to be **condemned to the 'waste bin'.**

It is no longer 'commercially viable' to provide the service due to the intrusive and overbearing effects of regulation, inspired and supported by those same politicians.

Credit unions offering even lower returns and poor facilities by comparison are the imposed substitute. **But who visits the depositor?**

When Financial Services Regulation was being discussed with Colette Bowe and her colleagues from the Personal Investment Authority in London, the impending plight of Friendly Societies and Industrial Branch Offices and the house calls of the Home Service agent were highlighted.

RURAL POVERTY

Colette Bowe cast them aside proclaiming **how inefficient these organisations were** and what poor value for money they were.

Rural Post Offices offer the same **meagre living for the operative** with similar local contact and concern for their patrons. The social aspects are ignored when it suits the argument.

Rural Post Offices **are inefficient** in some eyes, too. How much more inefficient to spend two million pounds on consultants that would have 'The Post Office' change its name to some incomprehensible gobbledygook that few will understand; and even less require.

Can the loss of perceived **self-determination** for the less well off ever be calculated? Those in poorer circumstances may **not want** some **prescriptive mechanism** dictated by political expediency and Civil Service logic. That is why **many shun the state benefits** that they are entitled to. There is **pride in self-determination**; many exhibit such pride.

They had a **trusted friend** to come to the house every week or every month week in, month in, week out and month out. They call no more. **The local 'Post Office' is trusted also.**

What is the **cost to society** of the alternative? The **politicians cannot tell you**. They seldom ask and the 'civil servants' care less.

Constant carping about high costs seems hardly the order of the day when the average earnings of these individuals was less than two-thirds of the national average wage.

91

Unions representing those in the cosy environment of large employers paying 'one and a half' and 'double' time, for 'unsociable hours and service to the nation', would do well to take a lesson from the lives of these fast disappearing **paragons of social service**.

The paid 'social servants' employed by local and national Government, with their substantial salaries, index linked earnings-related pensions, still manage to find time to get 'depressive illnesses' that get them time off with pay at the public's expense because the conditions that they meet with are so terribly undermining to their chosen profession's idea of Utopia.

The establishment has once again opted in favour of high expense, low return, and mediocrity to replace a social service that did not cost them a penny. The Welfare Reform Act can never replace what has been lost.

The argument is not 'dinosauric', it is catastrophic.

CHAPTER 12

BANKS AND BIG BUSINESS

When Canary Wharf went into liquidation the newspapers reported a deficit of **£600 million owed to the banks**. The money was lent to the developers of Canary Wharf at relatively advantageous rates of interest because, after all, this was an **asset backed development** and it was **easier to lend £600 million to one developer** than to a large number of small firms desperate for a £1,000 here, £5,000 there, £250,000 somewhere else.

When the banks do lend to small firms, the banks require belt and braces, **debentures and mortgages and three, four or five per cent over the 'base rate' plus** compulsory life insurance, plus compulsory critical illness cover, **plus, plus, plus.**

The rationale is that **small businesses are a higher risk than large businesses**.

There were approximately **24,000 bankruptcies in 1997**, which means that **£25,000** would have to have been lent to **each of those firms** to have the **same catastrophic effect as Canary Wharf**. It is also true to say that **the banks would recover 80 per cent of those loans to small businesses** in full. Not so from the liquidation of Canary Wharf.

It was reported at the close of 1999 that a major **'Direct' PEP and pensions provider had lost £14.4 million in the year.** The company handles hundreds of thousands of pounds of the public's money. They are still trading; **nobody has closed them down.**

Yet the **regulators close down several firms every month** because their **assets fall below the £10,000 capital** 'needed' to keep trading as financial advisers, even though they **never handle one penny of anyone else's money.**

Another 'smokescreen' using easy, almost helpless, targets for political capital. Another diversion from the main events.

LARGE BUSINESS BLUES

Environmentalists, quite rightly, ask for Government support in denying large supermarkets in particular, and other industries, access to 'greenfield' sites to **despoil yet more of our beautiful countryside**. Wal-Mart has recently purchased Asda, reportedly on the basis that they will be able to **develop more out-of-town sites**, as they have done in the USA. But equally, the other major retail superstores want large grass areas to build **vast car parks** to support their 'annihilation' zones.

Recently a commentator stated that a substantial supermarket chain paid out **£10 million in donations to 'good causes'** in one year. On the face of it one says "well done", but look behind the scenes. The PR department had also done a good job. **But what was the truth?**

Town centres, large and small, become boarded up or run down as the profit margins that allow the proprietors of those organisations **to eke out a modest living** become more and more constrained and less and less able to support the giving of service to their customers.

'Out-of-town developments' are part of the reason: along with **greedy myopic council officials.**

On the promise of a leisure centre, a new traffic system, or some cultural initiative, the local authority will **acquiesce to a new store, by Government decree**. The larger organisations have even been known to **buy the old council offices to get their own way**, and to get the council off a particular 'hook'.

THE GREAT GIVEAWAY 'CON TRICK'

And does this 'largesse' actually come from the large supermarkets that have their names emblazoned all over the paper as being so benevolent? Not on your life!

Most of it is 'extorted' from the suppliers of goods and services in exactly the same way as special promotions are, to give the impression that this giant organisation has some social conscience. It is the small to medium size business that provides <u>the supermarkets</u> with goods and services that are **coerced into paying into the charity fund**; **or lose the contract** that they have with the supermarket.

Producers that supply supermarkets are squeezed by the supermarket, with their stranglehold on the market place, to reduce their own trading margins, **to produce no profit on occasions**, and, on occasions, to eventually go out of business, to fund the 'largesse' of these 'supersize' customers. **The supermarket chain gets the credit whilst the suppliers take the strain.**

Anyone can write a cheque or two if they have the financial power to 'extract' the money from selected suppliers. The amounts are not small. Fifty thousand pound demands are not uncommon. **No new contract for the coming year is the ultimate sanction, and it is used!** Extortion today is a condition that is difficult to contract out of.

One producer of root vegetables at the end of the year was asked by a supermarket chain for a cheque in the sum of £50,000 or they would lose their contract. They refused to pay. They lost their contract. They also went out of business, which meant that their staff lost their jobs, the directors lost their investment and the property was sold for a pittance. The supermarket found a new 'sucker', sorry, supplier.

Another trick of the trade is to encourage buy-outs. One provider buys another provider 'out' until there are only two or three providers left in the market, then the pincer movement comes and in a trice, (well 10 to 15 years), **the supermarket management has gained all the expertise, cornered the market and captured all of the assets, at a knock-down price**.

ANYTHING BUT THE TARGET

Governments should see through the avarice, but they fail to. Instead, they are lured by talk of what will be provided, a playing field or computers, yes, we will do something to support this school, or, we will make some major road improvement, we will put a roundabout in or some traffic lights. Whatever will 'persuade' the administration is part of the 'game'.

In the financial services, or any other regulated industry, that form of 'bargaining' would attract a huge fine, censure or imprisonment. For a local authority it is beyond reproach for the 'betterment' of the community.

Take Sid as an example: Sid spent six months in prison for delivering whisky to managers of a large corporation as a Christmas 'thank you' for work between his firm and the corporation. There is an inconsistency in the two circumstances, which are not isolated 'one offs' but widespread practices.

Compare the actual value of the work done in the community by **proprietors of small businesses** and their employees. They are only able to do so through the returns that they make on giving services through their businesses.

A lot of this community service volunteer work is disappearing. Organisations such as Lions, Junior Chamber, Round Table and Rotary, are struggling for membership. Individuals are under financial and time constraints whilst Government, and substantial oligopolies are siphoning off their life-blood.

Large supermarkets may be able to give away £10 million but they deny two and three and four times that amount in physical effort, community spirit and social involvement.

Money buys materials. When it comes down to it, money measures very little in human terms. Our modern malaise is to see money, in and of itself, as a solution. Throwing money at a problem seldom resolves it. People resolve problems.

PROBLEM SOLVING

Jokes like this are just not funny. Whilst **regulators are preoccupied with trivia** that commerce and its consumers could sort out for themselves, **REAL PROBLEMS** on a huge scale are being **smokescreened** out of sight. Government 'quangos' 'burn' vast monetary budgets, and then reinvent themselves to burn some more.

Many is the time when reflecting on the story of **Robin Hood** that parallels in our modern day society emerge from the mist. But then, do we learn anything from the past?

Certainly there is a **Prince John around today;** you may remember that Prince John was left in charge when the King, his brother, went off to fight the crusades. Power got the better of Prince John and whilst power is good if exerted fairly and diplomatically, **absolute power is detrimental and corrupt.**

Prince John has a modern equivalent in **our Chancellor of the Exchequer**, a man who '**plunders** and then grants favours'.

Pension schemes and charities have had their special tax status on dividends from equities removed, drawing **£5.4 billion and £3.2 billion** out of their coffers **into the Treasury. Every year**.

The Chancellor then buys the offended individuals 'a beer' from the proceeds by way of a **Christmas bonus or 'Gift Aid'** and expects them to be grateful. 'Gift Aid' is metaphorically 'a beer'.

Increasing state pensions, along with pension 'tax concessions', is 'a beer': costing less than one tenth of the tax collected **from other people's pensions.**

Whilst shouting from the rooftops that "welfare and pension reform are on their way", the public were unaware of the level of 'spin' that was presented in that statement.

'SPIN' AND 'PRINCE JOHN'

The inference was that a positive pension regime would emerge from the initiative, but just like Prince John, the Chancellor got a well-measured routine worked out that in conjunction with his cohort would show an exercise of control reminiscent of his political forebear.

Robin Hood, you may remember, was fighting for 'right' having returned home to find his father had been murdered and his father's house plundered as a result of defaming gossip and of course, coincidentally, Robin Hood's **father's loyalty** to his King.

Businesses were brought to their knees by excessive 'tithes', which usually meant that the 'regulators' **demanded** a huge proportion of the **traders' merchandise** that then robbed them of their livelihood. Failure to comply (due to lack of goods or money in those days) resulted in their eyes being burned out, parts of limbs being removed, or death.

Incarceration cost money that was not available in those days. **One didn't want too many people in jail**. Sound familiar?

Legend tells us that good prevailed over evil in the end but one has to ask, at what cost? And at what personal risk to Robin Hood (Robin of Loxley). Robin Hood was a Saxon lord in a Norman environment. The weak are only weak because of the living they have to eke out. Given time and resources they can exert their will. Modern citizens have the time but **few exert themselves** to improve their personal position.

'Naming and shaming' is not new. The public pillory and the delight of many in society to view someone getting his 'comeuppance' is perhaps the most worrying trait of all. Our society seems obsessed with wallowing in other people's misery or misfortune: real or contrived.

The Jews, Kosovars, Hutus, have all been 'named and shamed'.

Without having watched the programme, the fevered excitement of those who did watch 'Big Brother' on television is disturbing.

98

The 'plot' glued television 'voyeurs' to the screen in what they felt was a great insight into people's lives. It illustrates the insatiable appetite of many to wish to enter into the lives of others to ridicule rather than praise them. The many soaps that regale our screens illustrate the same tendency.

It is not surprising then that many in society **accept blindly** that those who have been 'named and shamed' must have something to answer for. But is that so? Some well-known sports personalities may put you right.

PC NAMES BY ANY OTHER

Propaganda is not a word that one readily thinks of in our British Society and yet that is what 'spin' is. Our **'politically correct'** world calls any number of things names that they certainly are not and withdraws names from common usage because they might cause offence.

Propaganda is associated with dictatorial regimes whereas 'spin' is perhaps perceived as something entirely different. The 'spin' phenomenon has an almost indisputable **air of respectability**.

So it is that politicians and the media are locked into a constant information dialogue that vacillates between truth, half-truth, and downright fabrication. A **modern political leader IS AN ACTOR READING A SCRIPT.** Personal belief, it appears, should rarely be the basis of one's utterances. It may not serve the cause.

'Pensions mis-selling' falls very much into the 'spin' category as may fox hunting, which will be discussed later. **Charities have been deprived of a major source of income** by removal of the tax credits that were available on investments in stocks and shares, and yet those same charities are not taxed on interest arising from banks and building societies. Spin 'doctors', is that Dr. Jekyll or Mr. Hyde, direct the **'play on words'**.

Tax from deposits can still be reclaimed. The public understands interest and will therefore question the loss of any relief. The **public is confused by tax credits** on share holdings and therefore accepts, without question, any changes of tax treatment **by default**.

TAKE AND GIVE

Our latter day 'Prince John' heralds **an exchange of billions of pounds received for a few hundred thousand given back**, if that.

Whilst one acknowledges that the 'Gift Aid' scheme simplifies the old covenant scheme, does it really do that much to improve the position of the charities when compared to the destructive power of taking away their tax relief from them?

Dividends are a major source of their income - **£3.2 billion** per year clawback into the treasury – from charities. (**The emphasis must be on the word treasure** (treasury).)

Similarly with pension schemes.

Was **the erstwhile Paymaster General Geoffrey Robinson** right in his assertion that tax credits were a 'notional tax' and as it wasn't paid there was no sense in giving relief against it?

This is not so much a mathematical problem as an **arithmetic problem**, but it relates to expenditure 'above the line' and 'below the line'.

One concludes that the **Paymaster General** and his mandarins just simply **did not understand** the accounting process that dividends went through 'below the line' as opposed to interest payments made by banks and building societies that are 'above the line'. Or they relied upon public ignorance to **deliberately mislead them**.

'Above the line' merely means an expense against the income of a business. Interest payments come out before the net profit is declared. It is therefore easily seen in the accounts. If tax is paid on interest at source, that too is easily recognisable and repayable.

The situation with dividends is entirely different because dividends are essentially a distribution from the net profit of a company. Therefore the dividend is paid **after declaration of the net profit**. Tax is still payable on it and therefore tax relief is still relevant.

The letter to the Paymaster General and the reply, four months later, from his civil servants illustrates the ignorance that does not compensate for the damage that is done. These are not the outpourings from 'mandarins' but rather the sour taste from a bunch of 'lemons'.

This form of back door taxation is loathsome and despicable; because, of course, the effects **only come to light many years after** the Government that introduced it has ceased to be in power and its proponents are once again drawing their exemplary pension entitlement. The public pays both ways.

Perhaps the naming and shaming should be reversed as it was at Runnymede when **Prince John sealed the 'Magna Carta' after a 'popular' uprising.**

It seems that some people have a really hard time learning that ordinary citizens will only take so much 'spin' before they see through it, and react. And react they did in the 'fuel crisis', over prices.

THE EQUITABLE - 'DEL BOY' ANTIQUES

Watching the Antiques Road Show can be quite sobering on occasions when what appears to be 'good', turns out to be 'worthless' and what was **bought for a pittance at a car boot sale turns into thousands of pounds.**

It also brings to mind 'Del Boy' and 'Rodney', **knowing the price of everything and the value of nothing** is the limit of Del Boy's expertise, whereas Rodney, the fall guy, actually has that element of business acumen called **common sense and value recognition**.

Journalists some 10, or more, years ago heralded the Equitable Life as being the epitome of good value for money. The Equitable Life Assurance Company had 'no middle man' and apparently paid no commissions to those that sold its products.

The **journalists** are not eating **'humble pie'** now that their temple of consumer friendliness has ceased to take on new business; no, they merely accuse 'The Equitable' of management ineptitude.

There is nothing for nothing in the world. **Air is free at a price**. Ask anyone who goes sub-aqua diving.

The interesting thing about the Antiques Road Show is that even modern collectibles such as *Dan Dare* memorabilia, the *Dandy* and the *Beano* annuals or *Star Trek* models have taken on values well in excess of their original cost price and yet items of furniture, **which have actually cost thousands of pounds to produce, cannot be given away**. 'Equitable Life' is like the furniture in spirit only. Who wants it at the moment?

Such was the case with wooden bedsteads 15 years ago and those large ash and oak wardrobes. If they had not been cut up and burned, one could have bought them for £2.00 or £3.00 apiece.

GOOD VALUE, OR CHEAP

What has the foregoing got to do with 'Stakeholder' pensions?

Well arguably the Equitable, along with a number of other life assurance companies, do not make enough margin on their products. Like Del Boy, the management was always trying to convince everybody in the market place the **bargain basement was their domain**.

Remember the old barrow boys at the Saturday markets? Plant a few purchasers to 'sell' to, then once the crowd had been attracted with a no margin product, sell the 'high margin sub-standard stuff'.

What 'high margin stuff'? **This is not a Saturday market**, but the managers are acting as if it were.

These 'businesses' are being run on a relative shoe-string, "If modern technology, by way of the Internet, is employed, we will make a profit."

Some day, maybe never.

Mr Micawber, of David Copperfield fame can be loosely quoted:

"If you earn £20 and you spend £19.95 then you have a good business.

If, however, you have earnings of £20 and you spend £20.05 then you have misery and strife."

The Equitable provided the cheapest term insurance (for smokers), cheap Convertible Term Insurance and was set to sell cheap 'Stakeholder Pensions'.

The Equitable spent millions on advertising and fêting the press.

The company relied, at least until the Financial Services Act curtailed the insurer's activity, on the benevolence of their professional **policy-holders** to, in effect, **sell to new customers**. Everybody, it seems, has now got his or her just rewards for **financial ineptitude**.

We live in a consumerist society and the one thing that one knows about 'the consumerist' is that perceptions speak louder than facts. Remember 'Rolls Razor' and 'Court Line'? What about 'De Laurean'? Will Belfast ever forget?

Del Boy is portrayed running about in a 'Robin Reliant' van, itself worthy of a place on the Antiques Road Show.

FORTY YEARS OF LOSING MONEY

A similar motorised vehicle that has caught the imagination of the world is the **Austin Mini**. The Austin Mini, in more than 40 years of production, has failed to recover its manufacturing costs, despite its buoyant sales numbering hundreds of thousands.

There will be some marketing man somewhere telling 'the Board' that it was **worth losing the money** on sales to get the marvellous grand prominence in the market place that **makes Austin the name that it is today**.

A quote from a **Board member** was to the effect that they **made no money on the car but, "just look at how well they are selling!"**

'Stakeholder' is falling into exactly the same trap. It is the trap that Personal Equity Plans (PEPs), Corporate Estate Agencies and ISAs have 'pulled' the larger insurance companies into in the past.

The Marketing Department **convinces those who really should know better** that they will be able to **sell** higher margin products off the back of a **'loss leader' product**. Dream on. The financial markets do not work that way.

THE PROFIT MOTIVE

'Rodney' could tell 'Del Boy' a thing about that in their London suburb setting, which is only a microcosm of the international market, as you will appreciate.

What would a 40-year-old Austin Mini be valued at in the Antiques Road Show, assuming they dealt in neo-classic cars? In real terms: not a lot.

Muddle-minded politicians who impose charge caps on financial service contracts (1 per cent in the case of 'Stakeholder') in the belief that they are somehow going to influence the market place to the benefit of the consumers should perhaps **reflect upon the fate of British Leyland** when it was a **nationalised concern**.

The plight of **'The Dome'**, which was subjected to **a business plan befitting of Enid Blyton creation** (Big Ears did drive an Austin Mini didn't he?), and similar 'Government excursions' into commerce, give credence to the arguments that Government, at civil servant and politician levels, should **stay out of commercial activity**. The parlous state of the erstwhile soviet bloc countries is surely evidence enough.

The steel industry, the coal industry and numerous other examples show the aptitude of those who have no experience of business to carry the message of commerciality forward in a beneficial way.

The political mind has destroyed more commercially than it has ever grown to fruition, whatever its political hue. (Don't mention the Ground Nut scheme.)

CHAPTER 13

IF THE FACTS ELUDE YOU – MAKE IT UP

Black Adder, as we know, has a wry sense of humour and on so many occasions, with the aid of a well-produced script, his antics rebound on him in a perversely self-satisfying way. Self-satisfying for the viewer that is.

Whilst being adept at making fools of others, he invariably ends up with egg, and a fair smattering of someone else's breakfast, all over his face.

Had he been in charge of the financial services industry, his expertise in this matter would have been of great benefit.

HISTORICAL HOGWASH

Of course, 1594 is a long way from 1994 but it seems that **ineptitude transcends** time in a way that can only be marvelled at.

The powers that be would have taken *Black Adder* and *Baldrick* to one side and castigated them for mis-selling 'this' and inappropriately advising 'the other', would have forced *Black Adder*, as the employer, to compensate those that had been misled, by *Baldrick*, the salesman.

Such may have been the cost of the review and compensation exercise that the employer 'Adder Inc' would have to release *Baldrick* from his dubious duties as general 'dogsbody' and spend his own time and money and effort proving that he, *Black Adder* was not as inept as he was accused of being.

Black Adder would not have exhibited the incompetence, for the purpose of this supposition, *Baldrick* had. But *Black Adder* was **forced to pay the compensation and investigate the cases**. Very expensive. Very time-consuming.

EMPLOYER RESPONSIBILITY

In the meantime, *Baldrick*, freed from his master's contract of employment could swiftly become self-employed and under 'the rules' escape the entire overhead of investigating the work that he was responsible for under his previous employment. He could spend all of his time developing his business with new clients (and probably play golf, had it been invented, or **have the occasional joust**, himself).

We know that *Black Adder* can be fairly devious; but *Baldrick*?

Baldrick **would be free to do what he likes** in the market place, under the new rules, without any of the financial baggage, professional indemnity insurance problems, or the time cost in reviewing all of his old client base, that has all been retained by his previous lord and master. He would be as free as a bird. **Nothing has changed from 1598 to 1998**.

Those that were tied salesmen with the banks and the major 'opportunist' organisations, now disbanded, have all hit the streets devoting their time almost entirely to their clients' needs.

Like *Baldrick*, they have not a care in the world. They have **no 'baggage'** to divert them from their ability to earn.

Those that are established in the market place, as with the *Black Adder* caricature, are fettered with the **ball and chain of unnecessary 'reviews'** created by an overbearing bureaucracy that in many instances costs them their livelihood for no good reason; and **without one complaint being lodged against them** by one of their customers.

At least in *Black Adder's* time Queen Elizabeth I would have despatched the head quickly and finally; but for many in this latter-day Elizabethan era, **'death' is torturous, painful, extended yet inevitably, just as certain.**

ROLE REVERSAL

Imagine: The roles are now reversed. *Baldrick* has worked for 12 years and has **never been in contact with the public**. He could never have mis-sold to anyone. He is professionally qualified. He is **made redundant**.

The only thing that *Baldrick* knows is the financial services industry and he honestly believes that he can give service to society and earn a living in doing so; by continuing his profession and **investing his redundancy** money in the purchase of a small 'limited company' owned by *Black Adder* in a large rural county which he can operate as an independent. Our *Baldrick* is actually **a real person named Danny**.

OWNER – NO WAY OUT

Danny knows the community and a lot of the local professionals. In purchasing the company he had to **relinquish the existing client base to the previous owner** (who will operate through his second office with a renamed trading style **12 miles down the road)**.

Danny's wife and two children (neither of whom are in their teens yet) put the redundancy behind them and look forward to a fresh start, a new life and **a lot of hard work**.

Danny wakes one morning to find that a substantial package has arrived from the Personal Investment Authority (PIA), his regulator. They **require Danny** to analyse a whole raft of life assurance, investment and pension contracts which he had never come into contact with before (having worked for one company) arranged by the previous owner (*Black Adder*).

What the surprise package advised was that he had **to investigate**, at his own expense, **all of the personal pensions** sold to clients through the limited company he had purchased, but which were now looked after by the **ex-proprietor** of the business who is operating 12 miles away. He has no such responsibility even though he sold the products.

109

In *Baldrick* parlance, he, *Baldrick* has all of the financial responsibility in the 'Danny' situation whilst *Black Adder* has **cleverly passed it on** with the sale of the limited company that *Baldrick* purchased. In this situation it is *Black Adder* who is 'free and clear' to lead a normal life.

Does this seem fair? Furthermore, **does it seem real**?

Has there been a mistake? The regulators pointed to the rule book. Danny was lumbered with what turned out to be 21, Phase 1, pension sales to review. **Not one client had complained**.

Subsequently, all of the cases are **proved to be without fault** or defect and yet in time, effort and money, the exercise cost Danny £800 per case to review. 21 x £800 = **£16,800**. Just imagine some 'governing' body **forcing you to spend that amount of your family's income** on a fruitless exercise.

What needs to be considered at this point is that the **average earnings** of a life assurance salesman, which, according to LIMRA (which researches these things), were **£11,800 per year**. Average self-employed earnings are £12,600: (Central Statistical Office 1998) and average national earnings £18,400: (Central Statistical Office 1998): **Danny had no income.**

DO WHAT I SAY, NOT AS I DO

Failure to do the exercise would result in 'disciplinary action' and an arbitrary and extremely 'painful' fine.

This situation is not an hypothesis. **It actually happened**. Not just to one person but in different quantums, sets and circumstances **to a whole raft of people across the country**.

Danny became depressed: suicidal. His marriage was put under a huge strain and, of course, his ability to concentrate on actually conducting work and sorting out real problems for real people that might earn him a living was also impaired.

110

Twenty-one times £800 was more than **one and a half times Danny's expected net earnings** in an established working environment. <u>It is all off his 'bottom line'</u>. The 'bottom line' is what Danny hoped to use to pay for food and the **basic requirements of his family.**

Whilst we can guffaw with amusement at *Black Adder* and *Baldrick's* antics and perhaps even admit that - well, it is all fairly good humoured and **not really that harmful to anybody**, there is no such malevolent attitude to those who are **guilty until proven innocent**, and are forced to spend large amounts of their own resources, providing that proof of innocence, **in this day and age**.

OCCUPATIONAL PENSIONS: ARE THEY REALLY THAT GOOD?

Baldrick did not have a pension scheme and would, in all probability, have failed to achieve an age when it would be payable. He might just as well have worked for **the British Motor Corporation**.

It would be useful to run through a case history of someone in an occupational pension scheme that came with working for a very **substantial employer**, the British Motor Corporation (BMC).

It is useful to **'test the system'**. **That is what an engineer would do.** But not so an economist.

Just how informed were the Treasury about pension schemes and how interested were they in facts, rather than perception?

You remember BMC? Designer and builder of the 'Austin Mini'.

The ability to **'transfer' from occupational pension schemes** to personal pension schemes was brought in by the Conservative Government of 1986. Many of those employees served with redundancy notices in the late seventies through to the time of the changes in legislation were **dissatisfied with their employers' pension** entitlements. Interestingly the trustees were not subjected to public, or private, scrutiny.

The Government of that day's 'successor' Conservative Government started the **pension review in 1994**. Arguably political expediency has taken over since, as their political opponents at the time, those now in Government, wanted to '**rub** the Conservatives **nose in it'. At your expense.** Pensions should not be about politics.

NOT EVEN LOCKING THE STABLE DOOR

Where they had the opportunity to bring justice and create something of real benefit for the consumer, they have, through the utterings of **Patricia Hewitt (Treasury Minister)** and her predecessor **Helen Liddell MP** destroyed their own credibility. This latter lady shares a large part of **her history with Robert Maxwell** - the late chairman of Mirror Group newspapers.

His reported **'misappropriation' of pension fund money** is said to be the **catalyst for the pensions review**.

Insurance companies were conspicuous by their absence in the Maxwell affair (which is not quite the position of Helen Liddell - she worked alongside Maxwell). Does that explain her over-zealous attacks on everyone in financial services? **The Mirror Group Pension** was self-administered, it was **NOT AN ASSURED SCHEME**.

The mechanism by which Maxwell perpetrated his 'fraud' is still unchanged and available for anyone else to use IN THE NEW MILLENNIUM.

TWENTY-THREE BILLION POUNDS, of your money, **LATER. The pensions review has achieved little but political rhetoric and financial waste**. The happenings of recent times make *Black Adder* appear the most saintly of employers.

One has to acknowledge, and defend, 'defined benefit' pension schemes. Great Britain can be proud of its pensions heritage and the pensions industry that has grown, since the 1950s, to be the **envy of the world**.

But such things won't happen without pain and without occasionally developing problems. Of course, in the late 70s and early 80s problems started to manifest themselves as above average earning 'white collar' redundancies exposed 'inadequate' retained benefits in occupational pension arrangements. **Pension scheme pillaging was prevalent**.

DEFINED BENEFIT PENSIONS ARE BEST. REALLY?

This resulted, in 1986, **due to pressure from the media**, in a wholesale advertising campaign that prompted people to '**throw off the shackles of company sponsored pension schemes**' and '**take up their own.**' Working people could have their 'own pot' to move from employer to employer.

Jobs for life were no longer the order of the day in 1988, so we were informed.

The trade union movement had diminished in power and large employers reduced the size of their workforce. Redundancies had been well in evidence and, of course, Des, the case study, had fallen victim to much of that. Yet, when this case history was sent to the Treasury for Patricia Hewitt MP, as the Treasury Minister, to comment upon (in 1999) the reply was received:

"Well, we know all that, but things have now been changed so that they are better." One is tempted to ask, "better? In what way?"

OCCUPATIONAL PENSION SCHEME HISTORY

(as remunerative as the Mini)

Des was a member of the **BMC Pension Scheme from 1965**. At that time he was in his **early twenties**, was **not really that interested** in pensions, it was **compulsory** that he join the pension scheme and the **company paid nothing** towards the scheme at all. He alone contributed.

In **1967 Leyland purchased the company** and the BMC scheme was put to one side.

113

1968 there was a new scheme formed: the **BMH SCHEME** and the original money from **BMC was paid back** in cash which Des **then spent in the pub**.

He was in the **new scheme until 1973** and that scheme was called **British Motor Holdings**. And again all his money was **paid back**, the scheme operator, **the employer, paid nothing**.

That bought a new fridge.

He then entered into the realms of the **new, third, Leyland Scheme.** It had a lot more substance than the original but in **1982 he was made redundant**. His money was locked into that scheme. There **were no transfers out allowed**.

In **1982 the tractor division was sold** to Marshalls of Gainsborough and they had a **contributory scheme**, which he paid into. A **5 per cent contributory scheme.**

After three and a half years, Marshalls went into liquidation and it was **then found, in 1985** - December - it was Christmas when he was made redundant, that **Marshalls had not been paying** into the pension scheme and that the **pension trustees were therefore creditors of the company**. The scheme was owed the missing contributions.

The **scheme was operated by a bank;** Roytrust of Canada.

"Roytrust" was not interested in the pension scheme. Once there was **no more money coming into the scheme**, Des confirms, they were really not interested.

They **sold the scheme to Legal & General Assurance**. Bear in mind the **only contributions** that had been paid in were those **from the employees**.

Legal & General immediately sought to pay all of the contributions back to the employees, *less tax*, which Des refused to accept. In fact, he has still got the cheque, uncashed, for **£1,153, which represented his years** in that particular pension scheme.

The date is significant, 1986. In 1987 Des took some advice and moved his pension from Legal & General to **a Norwich Union Section 32**. It has grown reasonably well since then.

The **Leyland Scheme eventually became the Rover Scheme**.

That is fully **paid up.** That is the scheme he **was locked into**, you will recall.

Des was out of work for quite a while and then got a **job with GEC** as an engineer and currently works for GEC. He was a member of the **GEC Pension Scheme**.

However, that scheme **became defunct in March 1999** when GEC became 'Althom' of France and they set up **yet another UK Pension Scheme**.

The right question to ask is: given the track record of this individual in **blue chip companies** right the way through his employment history, no personal pensions in sight, would **you have joined the Occupational Pension Schemes and been satisfied with the result if you had had this history** as an engineer, to hand?

I think not.

WHY NOT ASK THE QUESTION?

Des's situation is reflected in thousands upon thousands of other individuals. Scanning the numerous pages of the Treasury Reports and the evidence given to the Treasury Select Committee nowhere will you find a 'Des' situation ever mentioned, let alone questioned.

Nowhere in authority has anyone really posed the question: **is an Occupational Pension Scheme good value for money on every occasion?** Does it really suit <u>every</u> individual? Young members do not receive the

115

benefit of an employer's contribution because it is not necessary. **The employee's contribution is MORE THAN IS NEEDED to pay for the benefits.**

Bear in mind that the **major banks, Sainsburys and other major institutions** are **switching** from Occupational Pension Schemes **to Group Personal Pensions**.

The personal pensions that individuals are currently being **coaxed out of** and back into the sort of scheme that Des became a derelict piece of flotsam from, on numerous occasions, will, in all probability, prove to be **better value and more trustworthy.**

DERELICTION OF DUTY

The Select Committee is guilty of a dereliction of duty not in asking the questions it has, but in **not asking the questions it should have.** If it really wants justice then it should remember the old biblical story about the **darnel growing in the field of wheat.**

A wise old sage in those days recognised that if you went into the field of wheat to pull out the darnel, **the damage that was done to the wheat crop**, as it was trodden underfoot in an attempt to achieve the impossible, was of **greater detriment than the offending weed.**

The whole **pensions review is a farce** that would do the West End of London proud, it has been running so long.

As **a test of the integrity of Phase 1** it would be **sensible** for the Select Committee to **appoint a totally independent individual** with the appropriate knowledge and skills to draw from the Personal Investment Authority (PIA) a **sample of thirty concluded cases** and run an assessment on them just to see whether it is going to be **value for money in carrying out Phase 2** or whether it is purely a political expediency to pull out the darnel at the expense of good wheat.

The Financial Services and Marketing Bill is inadequate in almost every respect. It is **inappropriate to couple banking with life insurance or pensions in one regulatory environment** unless properly qualified and 'time served' individuals are used for the regulatory process. They are entirely **different disciplines** requiring different mind sets and are appropriate in different circumstances.

MISPLACED REGULATION

Life insurance is not an investment and, therefore, whole life policies and term insurances **should not come under the aggressive regime of disclosure**. The amount of protection being put into force at the moment is diminishing because of the cost of providing it under the current regulatory system. The new Bill does little to alleviate that.

There is **nothing** that I have read that has a **semblance of credibility** in statistical terms to justify either the Act in its current form or the Financial Services Authority, which is a joke. The Financial Services Authority is run by **bankers and IMRO,** both of whom are reportedly **responsible** for the **largest frauds** in the last 10 years, the main one perpetrated by **Maxwell** and a close second by **Peter Clowes.**

It seems that **even Des has fallen foul of bankers attempting to do an insurance company's job.** They were only **interested in the money not in people** and that is the subtle difference between those who operate banks and those who operate *bona fide* life assurance and **pensions companies** whose primary **concern is people**.

When money is subject to a 'short-term view' it is the centre of attraction. When it is a 'long-term expediency', it pales into relative insignificance.

It is to be hoped that **the authorities** will **now** start to ask the correct questions of the correct people and **obtain statistical evidence**, which will be made readily available to see and **verify their assertions**. (Just a random choice in the same way as their inspectors would operate on a visit to, say, Danny's office.)

117

CHAPTER 14

REFLECTIONS OF REALITY

Are you a *Jonathon Creek* fan? Jonathan Creek is not everyone's cup of tea, but not being a detective and portraying a sort of *Colombo* figure **in a duffel coat** rather than a rather tacky 'Gannex' look alike, makes him quite intriguing. Couple that with that atrocious female who treats him so badly, then one can get quite sympathetic towards the super intelligent **master of magical illusion**, who seems fated to fail in matters of the opposite sex.

Politicians are masters of magical illusions as we all know, except that they do not always understand the trick it seems. It is much like the chap that Jonathon Creek works for. Of course television programmes have to be visually stimulating and so on, but **life can be the same,** don't you find?

Checking in the rear-view mirror to see how the world looks behind your car is particularly sensible if you are reversing, with your head facing forward.

REFLECTING ON CERTAINTY

Provided that you can **concentrate** on three mirrors, and the orientation of the steering wheel, at the same time as operating the foot pedal, which activates the brake or the accelerator and clutch, or in extreme circumstances all three, **you will succeed**.

'Pensions mis-selling' is one of **the best master tricks of mirror deflection** that one could ever come across.

The particular *Jonathon Creek* mystery that is described here has been repeated several times. Therefore the fact that **the woman** did not really **commit suicide**, even though her husband watched her do so by placing a **12 bore rifle to her head** and pulling the trigger, has much the same startling impact when one discovers that even though one has seen pages upon pages, probably by now millions of words expended, stating that those with

personal pensions have been **sold a pup**, the pup could actually turn out to be a **pedigree 'Crufts' winner.**

But how can this be you ask? Well it was all **achieved by mirrors**. The Jonathon Creek thing I mean.

You see the conservatory had windows onto a wide expanse of garden and the deceased woman's husband always sat in a particular chair in the conservatory. **He was an invalid.**

Now, I won't spoil the story, just in case you haven't seen it, by telling you who did it. The butler (oh blast) sorted 'the job' out by placing **a mirror** which had been part of a **previous trick** performed by the woman (a professional illusionist), into the clear glass of the conservatory.

Then, with the **angle of reflection equalling the angle of incidence** (now how is that for a run back into physics, my teacher would be proud of me) the 'gent' sitting in the chair would see a different part of the garden than that where his deceased wife actually lay.

Well, if you have seen it you will know which episode I am talking about and if you have not, the plot thickens. It is worth watching.

A PENSION PARALLEL

Pensions mis-selling uses the **same principle**, one merely deflects the view from one scene to another. In the 'pensions mis-selling' debacle it was a very clever trick by the **Securities and Investment Board**, who looked after banks and their subsidiaries, **deflecting the view** of the observer onto the life insurance industry. **Enter Jonathon Creek**, or someone else who understands how illusions are created, your author perhaps.

The plot is really very clever because the banks, having been subject to an **internal** Securities and Investment Board **review,** were found to have **short-circuited** a somewhat simple **sales process**. Instead of asking two basic questions:

120

A).   What **benefits do you have** under your existing pension scheme, or might be provided under a pension scheme that you have access to?

and

B).   **How much money** have you got in your company pension fund?

They merely asked the second question, **"how much money have you got in your company pension fund,"** and sold the individual a personal pension that fitted with the amount of money. That is not entirely bad, but it **is not entirely scientific** either.

It is not entirely bad because there is a 'chance' that the person concerned may have done better in the personal pension than they would have in the vaults of their employers' pension scheme, but of course if one is acting professionally it is always nice to know that the **projected benefits** at least have a 'chance' of **producing something akin** to the alternative; without knowledge of the alternative, that judgement could not be made.

INEFFECTIVE SENIOR REGULATOR

The Securities and Investment Board (SIB) **could not levy fines**. Therefore they could not fine the transgressors; they could merely request them to **"put things right"**. Which of course they did, **when the individual complained**.

Coincidental with the banks 'putting things right' some also entered into a set of circumstances that inexplicably **took rather more in interest charges** from, particularly it seems, **small business bank accounts,** than the interest rate being charged warranted.

Strangely, the **banks did not get disciplined** for that either, despite calls to politicians, although cases are well documented where £12,000 here, £6,000 there, £53,000 somewhere else, was eventually returned by the bank to those **account holders** astute enough to get experts in to check how much they were being **overcharged.**

That is another story and entirely too complex for the space available here. But it must have **filled up the coffers** whilst, at the other end of the corridor, they were being emptied **paying compensation**, without too much fuss, to those who complained about their pensions.

The metaphoric mirror went up, and **the focus was switched**, very cleverly, to the life assurance industry. Another useful **'smokescreen'**.

MAKING QUESTIONS COUNT

The mirror took the shape of **consultant accountants** being hired to do an **'independent assessment'** of **random files** held by life assurance companies and Independent Financial Advisers. One could assume that if one part of the financial services market was doing something 'disreputable' then the other part of the market was going to do much the same thing.

Just in case those then being the focus of attention were not as 'unsavoury' as expected, **10 times as many criteria** were introduced for examination. Provided a position could be established where more than half of the files are either 'suspect' or had 'inconclusive paper records' on those files then one could state that there **may have been 'a problem'**.

That is precisely what happened. **The politicians 'sat' as the disabled spouse in the Jonathon Creek incident**, in their 'chair' viewing the scene, they **saw what was intended** to be seen rather than what was actually there. Clever really. The outcome of course was commercial mayhem.

If you can make political capital why bother about examining the facts. The newspapers had created a server in the public domain by the *Financial Times* exposé, **'500,000 personal pension holders mis-sold'**.

The authors of the **KPMG report** (they were the accountants engaged to examine the life assurance industry files) stated categorically that their findings **only indicated that there was 'a lack of paper evidence'** to prove that the questions had been asked of those coming out of company pension schemes and moving their money away to a personal pension policy.

There was **a golden opportunity to make political capital** and an overwhelming case to say that **the pensions industry**, like the wife in the television drama, had merely **put a gun to its own head** and committed commercial suicide.

> **"They were culpable and they should be brought to book. They cannot avoid their responsibilities."**
>
> **Helen Liddell MP** (Quote – though not verbatim)

She, the Jonathan Creek 'wife', had committed suicide and it was a tragedy but now she should be put to rest.

The analogy is perfect. So of course is the incisive revelation of our amateur sleuth. Jonathon Creek never gets paid for any of these excursions into illusionary exposé, he only does it, seemingly, to create a story line for his disrespectful and abusive girlfriend. She is a journalist in the TV drama.

So what is the truth?

FOOLS RUSH IN

The truth is that **the life assurance industry had tried to warn of the oncoming calamity.**

Between 1986 and 1988 the **Government** in office **'forced the issue'** of making personal pensions available to a wider audience, removing the compulsion within employment of joining a company pension scheme.

The insurance companies voiced a view very strongly that the Government was 'opening' the market up too quickly because **systems were not in place** to deal with what they saw as a **massive marketing exercise that could go horribly wrong.**

Of course, if there is a stampede one cannot be left out. Particularly when it is a commercial stampede and it is perceived that a future livelihood depends on it. **The banks** and numerous **investment houses** were in full cry for the 'hunt'.

Everyone in the life assurance industry has known for years that the banks were seeking to capture a very significant portion of what they perceived as a very lucrative market for them to be in. **Lucrative to the banks, not necessarily to their customers.**

GEARING UP THE ASSETS

Banks have a responsibility to their shareholders. **Their customers**, as it has been proved recently by the closure of rural branches etcetera, are **merely an inconvenience**, which they will deal with at their leisure.

Banks are entitled to gear up their assets. They only **have £9.50 of assets** against **every £100 of liability**. There is an assumption that **only one in 11 people will ever come in for their money** at any moment in time. If everyone wanted their money out of the bank – 10 out of every 11 would get nothing. Oh it's true. Ask a banker.

Banks also started their own Unit Trusts. **Unit Trusts do not need significant assets at all.** They merely need nominal capital to start and everything else that they have is investors' money. They take a **management fee to pay for their overhead** and the rest goes into **their coffers**. Whoever owns the group makes the money. If it is a Banks Unit Trust operation then it goes back to the bank's bottom line and on to their shareholders. The same applies to OEICS.

By virtue of the fact then that £1 billion of assets gives £11 billion of muscle in the market place, banks are extremely strong. They are reportedly **providing Government with a whole economics analysis department free of charge** with significant numbers, 40, 50, 60 employees dedicated to the task. At least **two major banks provide the facility** and it is believed that others do so as well.

124

'One' has a fairly privileged position that close to Government.

The **life assurance industry** on the other hand has **£100 of assets to £100 of liability.** If they cannot maintain that margin then they have to go 'out of business'. **Equitable Life has ceased taking new business to protect, or retain, the ratio of assets against its liabilities.** That is perhaps why banks can buy insurance companies but insurance companies do not buy banks.

'SCENE' TO BE DONE

To return to the plot: **once the disabled individual in the conservatory had seen his spouse commit suicide**, the perpetrator of the deed wheeled him out of the conservatory to view the scene, unaided by mirrors this time. There she was, dead.

What the now distraught husband did not know was that the **perpetrator** of the original murder **enacted the suicide scene** that he had witnessed: dressed up as his spouse in a completely different part of the garden, as reflected in the mirror.

Now, whereas **the banks could not be fined**, the life assurance industry could, and of course fines are something that journalists love to report.

If **someone is fined** for a transgression then they **surely must have perpetrated the felony** for which they have been fined. This situation was created to 'tear the heart' out of an industry that needs £100 of assets against £100 of liability and has no other mechanism to recover the costs.

The life assurance industry could not do what the bankers did, put their charges up and take more money from accounts in interest than is actually due, their **premiums are fixed** at the point of inception of their policies.

125

A FINE MESS

The only money assurance companies have is the money from premiums and whatever they can generate from managing funds in the investment market place. But the market place was being forced into a more competitive situation all of the time.

Therefore, the receipts they were bringing in were, if anything, lower than they would need. A **heavy fine,** therefore, creates a situation where **assets and liabilities** are **out of synchronisation**.

The journalists, spurred on by self-seeking vested interest groups, looked further into **free asset ratios**.

Thus the perception **that Endowments and Pensions,** particularly from 'With-Profit Funds', were **going to deteriorate** in the long term, was **easy** enough to **promulgate. T**he whole situation "spirals down" and creates a position where mutual companies are vulnerable either to take over or **demutualisation:** which in turn makes them **easy prey; for – the banks**.

The villain should then get away 'scot-free' because he is 'distraught' and merely **seeks to console his master,** whereas the fact of the matter is that the butler (the man responsible for placing the mirror) is actually **responsible for a deed so heinous** that only the chanced finding of a clipping referring to the previous 'magic trick' exposed him for what he was. **Fiction sometimes outstrips** our own capacity for **rational thought concerning reality.**

A DICTATORIAL REGIME

The pensions review centred on 'pensions mis-selling' gave the opportunity to prove **whether justice or a dictatorship existed within the regulatory framework.**

Turning 'the searchlight' around the other way, the financial services practitioner, along with farmers who breed cattle, abattoirs that produce meat, teachers who teach kids and so on, was able to confirm that all are now

guilty until proven innocent. And that proof of innocence can cost a lot of money, time and effort. More importantly, the accusation can destroy or disfigure a reputation.

That is what modern regulation is **founded upon: character assassination - BIG TIME.**

The 'pensions mis-selling' review involved every financial adviser and insurance company examining its records to determine those individuals that had been sold personal pensions between 1988 and 1994 and establishing whether or not individual members of the public had been correctly advised in saving in that product. There were more than six million policy holders to scrutinise and contact.

This process **did not involve anyone making a complaint** to initiate the action. There was no question of anything being wrong or thought to be wrong by any individual, this was merely the **regulator determining that everybody was wrong until they were proven to be right**.

THE SHOE SELLER

Imagine that you sell shoes, or you are a local butcher or to give something that has some form of record, say a garage proprietor that has done motor repairs. You have never had any complaints, you work a full day and you just about make a living for yourself and your family, to maintain your lifestyle and look after the best interests of your customers, because you need their goodwill to stay in business.

You need customers to 'buy' again. It's odd, but **giving bad service seldom seems to lead to the long-term success of any business.**

The regulatory authority imposes the following regime, which has been 'adapted' to a more familiar set of circumstances. Buying a pair of shoes could be such a problem without proper regulation.

You might also bear in mind that at this stage 99.4 per cent of all businesses employ fewer than 20 people and many of the proprietors of those businesses take less home in their pay packet than their employees. Most of those businesses will not be sold. The proprietors relinquish any of their invested capital, when they come to retirement.

They will die 'in harness' or fade gently into obscurity. Those business owners are usually fiercely independent. They tend to do things 'their way'.

THE BIGGEST CONFIDENCE TRICK

Imagine, the regulator also insists that you waive your 'Statute of Limitation' legal rights (which precludes any investigation of a complaint about a service given prior to a six year period), and then insists on examining all of your records. Ordinarily, records must be kept for six years, then they can legally be destroyed.

You must reconstitute those records that have been destroyed: in your own time, and at your own expense, whilst still trying to maintain your business and current customer relationships and your level of earnings.

You will not do this within one set of criteria.

The individuals instructing you to do the exercise will continually change the rules. They have the capacity of judge, jury and executioner. You will have no right to question any of their decisions (although you may attend meetings that appear to give you that right).

With kind acknowledgement to the author – whoever he/she may be

"I'd like to buy a pair of black leather shoes, please."

"Sir, if only it were that simple. Here's my card and here's your Buyer's Guide."

"What's this for?"

"It tells you that I can only talk to you about shoes and allied products sold by this shop. I can't talk to you about shoes sold by any other shoe shop, nor can I give you any advice on, say, sausages for instance."

"I see."

"Probably the best way to proceed is to show you where we fit into the footwear industry. We buy in most of our products from the Far East at a fairly modest price and sell them on to the public at a considerably higher price; but, of course, out of the mark-up we have to pay for transportation, import duties, rent and rates, display staff, sales staff, cleaners and administration, etc., etc. And, of course, our shareholders have to be paid a dividend out of the remaining profits. Not many people think about this when they buy their shoes, but we think it's important, so, with this in mind, I'd like to ask you a few questions to make sure you get the shoes – or even the boots – that are <u>exactly</u> right for you. It may be that when I have all the facts I might recommend that you do not buy my footwear at all. May I proceed?"

"What do you want to know?"

"Well, how many arms and legs have you got for a start?"

"What have arms got to do with shoes?"

"Well sir, if, for example, you had only one arm and I sold you a pair of shoes with laces then that could be construed as bad advice by BASTIRO."

"Who's BASTIRO?"

"The Boot and Shoe Trade & Industry Regulatory Organisation."

"What would they do?"

"Put the boot in. A friend of mine had to leave the industry."

"What did he do wrong?"

"Sold a pair of carpet slippers."

"What's wrong with that?"

"Turned out the guy hadn't got a carpet. So you see, I need to build up a full picture of you. For example, do you need the shoes for business or pleasure or business and pleasure? How many shoes have you got already? How many casuals, suede, plimsolls, sandals, wellingtons, etc. do you

own? How many suits and what colours are they? Have you got athlete's foot? Can you touch your toes? Any corns or bunions or has your family a history of footrot? What kind of socks do you wear? How often do you clip your toe-nails? How much do you earn and what's your overall clothes budget... Well, thankyou for that information. I'll give it some serious thought and would you like to come back in two weeks' time."

Two weeks later...

"Ah, good morning sir. I've given it some thought, and what you need is a pair of black leather shoes."

"Wasn't that what I asked for in the first place?"

"With respect, sir, you have had the benefit of my professional advice based upon all the relevant facts as given and you now know with some certainty that you require black leather shoes. All the guesswork's been taken out of it. Here's your Reason Why letter – I recommend you buy these black leather shoes because they'll keep you feet dry, match your suits, look smart and you can afford them."

"Well I'm glad that's settled."

"So you want the shoes then."

"Yes please."

"Right, if you'd like to complete this application form and here's your quotation I'd like you to sign. It shows a complete breakdown of costs and profits and includes my 24 pence commission. Your product particulars describe in great detail how the shoes are made and the 'key features' are a summary of the product particulars, highlighting the risk factors."

"Risk factors."

"Yes. For example, if you live too long, the shoes may need repairing. On the other hand, if you die before you've had your wear out of them, I'm afraid there'll be no refund, even if they don't fit another member of your family."

"I see."

"So, just to recap: You've got my card, your Buyer's Guide, product particulars, key features, quotation, reason why letter. Now sir, you will get a letter from my Head Office telling you that I do in fact work for this company and also a cooling off notice. You can return the shoes within 14 days and have a full refund if you don't like them for any reason. Incidentally, how are you paying?"

"Cash."

"Ah! Well would you mind nipping home for a gas bill or something to prove your identity as you are not known to me. One last thing, sir; do any of your friends require shoes...?"

129

CHAPTER 15

JOBS FOR THE 'GIRLS'

Now, what you may not have been told about the EU is that every politician who succeeds in getting elected also succeeds in gaining access to what one can only refer to as a place in the **'Palace of Grand Retirement'**. Each member of the European Parliament is privileged to receive a pension amounting to a large proportion of the salary they were receiving whilst an MEP, for the rest of their life, **index linked of course.**

Now that is a job worth having.

Some would say that four years' pension entitlement would be more than enough, but a **pension amounting to 50 per cent of salary? And who pays for it?**

CHALLENGING "THE UNTOUCHABLES"

The Euro **MP cannot be pursued** for getting 'it' wrong. The only thing that one can do with them is vote them out at the next election, which may be several years hence. As we have seen, they can preside over the greatest travesties that man could possibly fantasise about and still come out 'smelling of roses'.

Every now and again the absurd **has to be challenged,** and I would guess that **NOW is about that time**.

Ordinary people going about their ordinary occupations, endeavouring to earn a living, are being penalised, bullied and driven to the depths of despair by bureaucratic overload.

There are those who have had the good fortune to have a good education, the wit to learn and continue learning. Those individuals have the ability and tenacity to question and hold forth against arguments that have been put to the public as 'fact'; yet turned out to be as mythical as the characters read about in fairy stories.

A SIMPLE INSIGHT

Reflect on one of the early counter oppressive regulation campaigns, when **a copy of 'Chicken Licken'** was sent to every politician involved with financial services, together with the regulators, in an endeavour to 'shock' them into a realisation that what they were doing was wrong and that **what they perceived as good regulation was not founded on fact.**

'Chicken Licken' is an interesting story. *Ladybird* still produce the book at less than £3.00 a copy. It makes excellent reading.

'Chicken Licken' was a chick. **Immature, inexperienced and unworldly** but highly intelligent. An acorn fell on 'Chicken Licken's' head. **'Chicken Licken' assumed that the sky was falling.** This 'catastrophe' had to be reported to the King, and so the saga started.

It continued its momentum as other characters in the book joined with 'Chicken Licken' in a flurry of feathers and intensely hurried activity to carry the message to the King.

'Chicken Licken', 'Clucky Lucky', 'Ducky Lucky', 'Goosy Loosy', 'Turkey Lurkey', all joined in the throng, running, flapping, calling out loud as they went, until, of course, **they met 'Foxy Loxy'.**

I hate to spoil the end of the story as I am sure that you would like to read it, but I guess that it doesn't take a lot of intelligent thought does it?

The fox said that he knew where the King was and that he would lead the distraught group to meet him. Of course, he took the whole ensemble home to his vixen and cubs. They had a wonderful meal (the foxes that is). Not 'Chicken Licken' and his companions. **They** were the **meal**.

And so it is with regulation. Few facts, plenty of action. Perception, woolly headedness, running hither and yon, gathering people together **who do not ask** the important question "**what makes you think that?**"

That was the question that was put in each copy of 'Chicken Licken' when it was sent out.

WHAT MAKES YOU THINK THAT?

Albert Einstein said, "always ask why."

Only two MPs bothered to comment.

One did not understand the book.

DEATH IS A CONSEQUENCE OF LIFE

The other one said that his son **really enjoyed 'Chicken Licken' getting eaten by the fox!** Doesn't that tell you something about the mentality of those who run our country.

No, I don't deride them. They have their own thoughts and their own agendas. Surely, however, it would make sense for them to **ask the question "what makes you think that?"** Would they instruct their children to act without questioning the decision to do so?

When conducting a debate it is better to understand all aspects of the discussion. With the benefit of all the facts the question, "what makes you think that?" can be answered properly.

You see, if only politicians had brains there would be no problem because we would not know that we have to be concerned. Us 'mere mortals' would merely fall in line and 'go with the flow', and follow the politicians' lead. Many citizens do that.

Fortunately, it **is not** only politicians who do have brains. It is just that **they seem to think that ours are inadequate for us to look after ourselves**.

133

Seemingly, in their view, **we are incapable** of providing them with any useful information that can be helpful to the cause of keeping humanity on an even keel. When they do ask, **they ignore the retort unless it agrees** with their preconception. Such arrogance is questionable.

Seemingly, every thought we do have is for our own divisive, self-interest. That submission is diametrically opposite to what most would perceive as being the truth.

The politicians, on the other hand, have no such bias. Everything that they do has to be seen as being for **the good of humanity**, because humanity is incapable of looking after itself.

Like 'Chicken Licken', all those with authority simply need is a tap on the head and they immediately respond as if **'the sky is falling.'**

That is exactly what happens to farmers, abattoir owners, restauranteurs, publicans, animal breeders and those in the financial services industry. 'Chicken Licken' is out in front causing such a fuss, something must be wrong. **It is all a decoy mechanism that avoids the focus being concentrated upon what really should be debated and attended to.**

A POISONED CHALICE

Wood and silver are amazing materials. Amazing because they are self-cleansing. Nature's own antibacterial materials for the manufacture of utensils.

Humanity has instinctively **known for many thousands of years**, that silver utensils had special properties in that contagious conditions were not spread. The **communion chalice is an enduring example**. That is why silver is so important in 'the church'.

Silver cutlery and drinking implements are **self-purifying**. That is one reason for communion chalices being made from silver, to avoid cross contamination as the 'cup' is circulated.

By the time the chalice has been turned after each communicant has taken wine, the edge of the **vessel is naturally 'cleansed' for the next recipient**. The use of the material is for utility not swank. Pottery replacements are a liability rather than the 'egalitarian leveller' that their introducers believe them to be.

Yet there are examples of false logic creeping through the liturgical corridors as unquestioning promoters of a less 'ostentatious' religious fervour endanger their flock by using cheap substitutes. **The 'church' cannot be seen to be affluent** – even at the expense, in every sense, of **natural hygiene**.

Natural wood has the same naturally sanitising properties.

Why was it then, that some years ago a directive was introduced from Brussels, supported by our own Government, to <u>**eject and destroy**</u> all <u>**wooden chopping blocks**</u> and replace them with artificially produced, often plastic, replicas?

A CHIP OFF THE OLD BLOCK - ANOTHER ILLUSION?

Perhaps if politicians had thought it through they may have detected just a hint of **commercial interest**. Perhaps they would have **seen through** the **environmental rhetoric** and recognised the fact that there are people in this world who will use perceived 'good' to fight genuine good.

It is the easiest thing in the world for those with evil intent to juxtapose one positive and align it with another positive and against all mathematical principles inveigle it to create a negative.

Take a microscope and examine the knife cuts in that Formica or plastic chopping board that you have and compare it to the crevices in your wooden chopping board and you will find the **wood pretty well devoid of bacteria,**

135

where the artificial board will be teeming with all sorts of microscopic organisms. Cuts in the **wood self-heal**, ask a butcher. Cuts in **artificial surfaces fester**.

Of course, one would use **bleaches and detergents, commercially produced**, to keep those plasticised surfaces clean.

Water is all that is needed for the wooden variety of chopping board, with a good **stiff, bristle brush**. Not much profit or political mileage in that combination to keep anyone other than 'Kleeneze' going, let alone a thriving Government **Health and Safety Executive**.

One should not underestimate the **costs**. The domestic bills for chemical bleaches, cleaners, rubber gloves (to avoid dermatitis and general skin maladies) together with the cosmetic 'repair and reconditioning kit' of special hand creams and balms, is **no small sum**.

A large prison kitchen had a facelift, which left it with a seamless, stainless steel servery that would be the envy of many just for its sheer beauty and aesthetic appeal. But is it really any more efficient when dealing with bacteria as a surface to prepare food on or to serve it from?

The kitchen staff have to use boards to avoid blunting their knives or damaging the surfaces. Wooden surfaces complement the cutting edge of the knife.

Re-enter the wood substitute, plastic. The chemicals required to ensure a sanitised surface then require special treatment as they enter the sewage system: another environmental problem has to be solved. **An ecological disaster area of Government making**. All **for the want of a small amount of research** before the destructive diktat was released.

Experiments in several universities revealed that **almost all bacteria are destroyed** by the enzymes inherent in natural wooden surfaces **within 60 seconds**. Silver is similarly self-cleansing.

Bureaucracy, which reacted so swiftly to remove wood from butchers, together with restaurant and grocers' food preparation areas, is now having to **admit it was wrong**. But at what cost? What huge cost? **Who paid the price** of this experiment? NOT the bureaucrats. **You!**

EXPERIMENTATION AFTER THE FACT

Would it not have been more prudent to **conduct the experiments <u>before</u>** making what appears to have been a popularist, perceptive decision supported largely by vested interest that produced the plastic products and the chemicals that industry and housewives have to use?

Media supported emotional blackmail seems inexorably to prevail over basic 'common sense'. **It makes a 'good' story, and that is just what it is, a story: pure fiction.**

The ever-gullible media is 'used' by the authorities or commercial PR departments, to propound the most preposterous theories. The 'young buck' national journalist can only progress 'on the back' of **a timely 'scoop' that has all the emotive drama of a Shakespearean epic and the mystical backdrop of a Paul Daniels' illusion.** A privileged leak must be so tempting. Something 'out of the norm' is so inviting.

How many can remember **wood shavings on the butcher's floor**? It was not there by chance. Why not use straw or rush matting?

Wood shavings actually sterilised the area, soaking up the blood adhering to the small off-cuts of meat, killing harmful bacteria. It looked unsightly but one should question the incidence of food poisoning in those days with the incidence today. **The topic under discussion is hygiene not clinical beauty.**

Plastic and stainless steel 'look' so fresh and clean. How perceptions deceive.

137

JOIN THE RIVER POLICE

Regulation is not simply a question of Dorrell's faux pas, or Curry's eggs (**no more Curry's eggs for me!**) with apologies to Major Bloodnock.

The Financial Services Authority and its forebear the Personal Investment Authority (PIA), are strategically located near the banks of the River Thames.

With the Goon Show in mind, one could almost hear the adjudicating disciplinary committee in number 25 asking the inevitable Goonish question:

"how would you like to join the river police?"

To which, of course, the reply is a projectile 'whistle' followed by a high dive 'splash!' and Blue Bottle's plaintive cry:

"you rotten swine, you have deaded me."

Of course, such Goonish humour for those of you old enough, and mentally unstable enough, to have enjoyed the wit, has little place in this rather engaging scenario. But the outcome is similar, **a dictatorial and overbearing officialdom** that dispenses justice with Goonish end results. The elimination of yet another business as it too 'joins the river police'.

Take the question of **the missing letters**. Well, they weren't missing really, they were only missing in that they had **never been sent**. Rather like the missing No 10 Downing Street episode of the Goon Show, a figment of creative imagination.

TWO INCONSEQUENTIAL LETTERS

This particular unsuspecting Independent Financial Adviser (IFA) had been obliged under the 'pensions mis-selling' legislation to **waive** his **six year statutory rights** to immunity from persecution (sorry, prosecution) and

138

examine files which under that statutory legislation the IFA had no obligation to keep, and, therefore, could well have destroyed.

The IFA was required to send out two letters before 31st December 1997 in accordance with **regulatory guidance**. The letters were a final act in a regulatory process known as the pensions review phase one.

So much importance was placed on the sending of these two letters by the appointed date that the offence of not sending them was deemed to be a major regulatory disciplinary actionable offence.

The contents of the two letters were **prescribed by the regulator** to ensure that having carried out the equally prescriptive task of examining files to establish whether one had sold a personal pension; one should then write to the POLICY HOLDER by the **designated date** of 31st December, 1997 and tell them that that was what one had done.

In short, the individual should be notified that the adviser had in fact followed the **correct course of action** in advising the policy holder to take out their personal pension.

RULES OR 'GUIDANCE'

Notwithstanding the basic **'rules'**, the regulator issued regular 'instructions' and additional **'guidance'** updating, amending and altering the original 'rules'. It was nothing to receive in excess of 60 or 70 **closely typed pieces of paper** from the regulator within a space of **six or seven weeks**.

As interesting as the regulator's literature is, in **no way** does the guidance support the business of **earning any income**. Overheads, as I am sure you will appreciate, do not go away. Overdrafts have to be paid, children fed, spouses kept and so on.

THE BIZARRE COMEDY

It was not surprising then that many IFAs actually found the going too tough. Their **balance of assets and liabilities** failed to meet the regulator's

139

requirements and the business was forced to close.   The ability of the individual **to earn a living was arbitrarily withdrawn.**

They had effectively **'joined the river police'.**

Reflecting on the *Goon Show* and the incredible humour that was borne out of everyday life, one could almost hear Moriarty and Grip Pype Thyne plotting in the background in the midst of **some dastardly deed.**

Visualise, if you will, the Independent Financial Adviser going about the various tasks that brighten up his everyday life, and a PIA inspector with that 'Grip Pype' voice enters the premises:

"Now then Neddy, what have you been up to?"

And the flustered Ned Seegoon; as our unsuspecting hero makes one of those all time classic statements:

"I'm spotted."

To which Grip Pype replies;

"Neddy why are you wearing that leopard skin?"

And then comes the inevitable, corny reply;

"so that is why I am spotted."

The PIA/FSA are **masters of the obvious.**

Returning to the case of the two un-sent letters in March 1998, the PIA observed that this final act in the pensions review was three months later than prescribed in 'the rules'.

One of these 'transfer' chaps was a company director who went through a traumatic divorce that left his ex-wife as chairman of the company that previously employed him as a director, **as a trustee of his Pension Scheme.**

He transferred his money out of the Pension Scheme for **safe keeping** and peace of mind; which was just as well, because the company subsequently got into financial difficulties and his position could well have been compromised.

In the event, he was decidedly better off by having completed the transfer as his funds were secure and, as it turned out, **generated far better benefits than the company scheme would have been able to do.**

The other case was even more interesting because this particular individual arrived at work one morning to find that **the contents** of his desk had been **cleared** into an executive bag with the name of one of the major supermarkets on the side.

He was asked for his car key, his office key, and instructed to leave the building. He had done nothing wrong. **His job just did not exist any more.** He had been made redundant because the company had very severe financial difficulties. He was the Sales Director and they had nothing to sell.

He, like many others, felt that in the circumstances, the Occupational Scheme that held the key to his retirement was an **inappropriate place** for him to now keep his meagre, though very important, resources. **His erstwhile director colleagues were the trustees in charge of his pension fund monies.** He transferred those benefits out into a private pension. For the technocrats who are reading this, both of these cases were Section 32 cases.

John retired in February 1998 with a pension that was a good **70 per cent above** what he would have **originally received from his company pension**. As you can imagine, retiring in February, the IFA concerned was well involved with the paperwork etc., in November and December of the previous year.

DAMAGING INNUENDO

Both of these individuals **were delighted** with what had been done for them.

Unfortunately in reading the rules, which one had to interpret oneself, the IFA misconstrued the vague instructions. If one phoned the 'help line', the helpful call centre guru referred one back to the rules and the interpretation process.

The rules were on this occasion misinterpreted.

The partner of the firm of IFAs responsible for **compliance had carried out all of the appropriate functions for reviewing the cases** and completed the reviews before the appointed date, the 31st December, 1997.

What the partner had not done was to write prior to that date to tell both of these individuals that they were better off having taken the action that they had taken.

Incidentally, **at no point was a complaint raised by either of the individuals.** In fact, neither of them wanted the IFA to spend time and money (at least £1,000 per case) on reviewing the situation.

Both were well satisfied. The first of the two had opted out of society altogether and joined a 'commune' in the south of England, so disillusioned had he become with society. He was so content with life that **the IFA eventually had to resort to phoning the DSS to locate the client's whereabouts**.

Enter, then, Grip Pype.

"Now then Neddy what have you been up to?"

And of course, having looked at the documentation he noticed that the 'return' completed by the IFA under the column; "have you sent out these particular letters?" the IFA had answered "no". Honesty demands one to say 'no' when that is the correct answer.

Therefore, it becomes even more astounding that **the resultant fine for not having sent those two letters** out was £4,000. Yes, **£4,000.**

The inspector reported to the Disciplinary Committee. The Disciplinary Committee adjudicated. They then wrote to tell the IFA that there had been a transgression of the rules and **that technically the pensions review had not been completed within the appropriate time:**

"Now then Neddy, you've been a naughty Neddy."

Grip Pype Thyne at his very best.

THE FINAL ACT

As has already been explained, the review had in fact been completed within the timescale set, with the exception of one prescribed 'action', which was the subject of some misinterpretation of the 'guidance notes'.

The letter, which, it was admitted by the authority, **had no adverse effect** whatsoever on its potential recipient, had not been sent, therefore, the **disciplinary phraseology** was released to the press that:

> **"the review had not been carried out and completed by 3lst December, 1997."**

Surely this was more of an 'i' dotting observation than a major transgression by somebody deliberately trying to avoid responsibility for a callous and self-centred act?

What followed had an air of unreality about it. It was as if Grip Pype and Moriarty had walked back into the IFA's premises and uttered the immortal words:

    **"Now then Neddy, open your wallet, and repeat after me:
help yourself."**

The regulator stated afterwards that because they **had access to the
accounts of every member** of the regulated fraternity (and, of course, could
stop them trading if they did not pay the fine), they would **never serve
notice of a fine** that would immediately, at least, **result in the bankruptcy
of the firm concerned**. Generous to a fault.

CHAPTER 16

KEEPING UP APPEARANCES

Where is the balance between good and evil, of sensible 'regulation' and 'over-regulation'?

Where is the justification for irrational bureaucracy and an overbearing, overburdensome cost on society, with dubious benefits? Where does one draw the line?

Surely the benefits derived must constitute **a greater value** than the cost of the exercise or the exercise is worthless.

A NECESSARY PROFIT

Caroline Instance, the Chief Executive Officer of OPRA, the regulator that looks after occupational pension schemes, recently stated, at a National Association of Pension Funds Managers conference that: **'Stakeholder'**, the new state proposed **commercial pension** arrangement was **not designed** for anyone to make a **profit** from.

The purpose of being in business is to make a profit. The whole reason for commerce is to sell goods and services **for a return**. Philanthropy is all very laudable but those who propound its virtues usually have a secure source of income.

For those who have moved house on a 'rag-and-bone-man's' cart in their teens, or been forced to sell their furniture to make ends meet, selling goods and services for a **profit makes good sense**. Ms Instance obviously has too high a salary coupled to an excellent pension scheme to concern herself with such a minor detail. Those whom she purports to 'protect' seldom exhibit her level of security.

'Stakeholder pensions', or any other product or service, have to be provided with **benefit to the consumer** as an objective but, with an over-riding element of acceptance that those who operate the schemes and provide those benefits do not do so out of the goodness of their hearts. They have families to feed, computer systems to replace, staff to pay, and of course regulators to support in an ever-increasing quantum.

For a regulator to be that naïve begs the question of how on earth they are qualified to regulate.

Of course Ms Instance may have had her comment taken out of context, knowing **those scurrilous journalists** and the way they can manipulate words.

AGRICULTURAL PRICES

Our acceptance that **proprietors** are expected to **work for nothing** manifests itself in the early years of the new millennium in agriculture more profoundly than anywhere else. Such is the global power of a very few dealers and distributors that those who actually produce the crops to be sold on a world-wide basis are now receiving prices for those crops that are:

a)   **less than it costs to grow** them, and

b)   **less than** they were **25 years ago**.

Whilst one accepts that televisions are cheaper, in real terms, than they were some years ago, in common with other manufactured goods, crop productivity reaches an optimum.

A sensible return for the effort employed in producing crops has to be awarded at a satisfactory level. Employees are not expected to work for less than the minimum wage. Why should those that carry the **burden of risk** deserve any less?

146

Farming is lonely. It is physically demanding, intensely uncertain because of weather patterns and disease, hugely dependent upon good management, and has the highest suicide rate of any occupation. The **return on capital employed is paltry.**

Commentators on the 'Jarrow Cavalcade' of fuel protesters, going from Teeside to London, compared the event to the Jarrow March:

> "We can see **no poverty there,**" was the comment from one 'old stager', as large tractors and articulated heavy goods vehicles processed down the A1.

How sad that such people do not realise **the huge monthly payments** that are committed for those vehicles and the hours of work that it needs to meet that commitment.

A recent survey showed that 37 per cent of all 'small businesses' (SME) operators, self-employed and mini limited companies were in **survival** mode (*Federation of Small Businesses*). They work in the hope of **making enough to survive.**

How callous we have become in our opulent society in prejudging others whose circumstances we know little of.

KEEPING UP

Comparing these 'real life' people to *Onslow* and *Mrs Bucket* (Bouquet) on the television, we see the paradox of our modern society. A **middle-class image** so often exemplified by those who judge others by what they appear to have; whilst at the same time rushing headlong to support those who outwardly appear to have nothing, when the truth of the matter is entirely the opposite.

Business people need the trappings of business because they are the tools of their trade, and **customers only deal** with those that they perceive **as permanent or secure.**

A 'Volvo F70' Truck, or a 'John Deer' tractor unit that will pull a multi-blade plough, is not evidence that the owner has more than £100,000 available to invest in the vehicle. It merely means that the business can get enough work for the vehicle to do, and produce enough top line profit such that, 'at the end of the day', it can **afford the repayments**. The proprietors may also be left with sufficient 'bottom line' profit to live on.

Unfortunately, the misapprehension does not just fall to the Caroline Instance's of this world.

Buyers, particularly those that purchase for supermarkets and large 'chains', are well versed in the art of 'commercial coercion' (some might term their practice 'industrial blackmail'), when they know that a **crop cannot be put back into the ground**, nor 100,000 items of a product, made to the buyer's specification, sold elsewhere into the market place.

It is easy to be like *Onslow* and **stay in bed** or 'stuck in front of the television' expecting the world to 'owe you a living'. And of course 'the world' proves the point by, on occasions, paying you the living that you expect.

It is also very easy to be like *Mrs Bouquet*, sorry *Bucket*, when you have somebody like *Richard* to run around after you and provide the wherewithal for your 'flights of fancy'. The real world has the *Onslows* and *Buckets* in it, but the **majority of people are entirely normal.**

NOT LIKE THAT AT ALL

Just as *The Thin Blue Line* or *Morse* bear little resemblance to what actually goes on in the police force, one has to treat the myth of every businessperson, being out to 'rip' every penny from your pocket they can, with **caution**. It is a failure to understand reality. Every business relies on the repeat custom of those it serves. **'Rip off Britain'** is more a product of an **inventive**, and spiteful, political **mind** than fact.

Whilst supermarket chains **tell 'us'** that it is the consumers who want **'two-inch-round potatoes'**, or 'eight-inch-diameter cauliflowers', what the consumer does not want is the **chemicals** that are used to produce the **2-inch-round crop of tubers** administered by the farmers who grow them.

Nor, perhaps, does she wish to acknowledge the fact that there is only a seven- to ten-day window whilst a crop of cauliflowers meets the 8-inch specification required of the grower by the purchaser.

What most housewives would be appalled to know is that if the **supermarket** decides **not to buy** the cauliflowers, lettuce or other crop during that time when the produce meets their size (or other) specification, even though they may have a 'contract' to buy the crop, they leave the farmer with no choice but to **plough the vegetables into the ground** for **no remuneration** when the crop is 'oversize'.

That is not business, it is 'corruption'. It is not fair dealing; it could easily be seen as 'blackmail'. The public are mere pawns in a game which a very few are privileged to come out 'winning', pretty well every time.

Like *Mrs Bucket*, we can perhaps have too much of a good thing and fail to question how we come by it, or perhaps be like *Onslow* and have no motivation or driving force to do anything for ourselves, or genuinely concern ourselves with the plight of others.

Either way, it creates the myth that living life is easy and that goods and services can be provided at less than 'cost'. **They cannot.**

We all need to question our motives and expectations when we buy and set that against what we expect when we sell, even if our only 'sale' is our integrity and our labour.

A BIT ON THE SIDE

The Consumers' Association recently accused the motor industry of profiteering. **How do you 'profiteer' and lose £2 million a day?**

Reality seems to be something that we, as a society, have ceased to take any note of. Like *Onslow* **and his deluded sister-in-law**, come down to earth. **The pleasures will be short-lived**.

It is difficult to know whether the head of a regulatory organisation like OPRA or of the Financial Services Authority, or the Rail Regulator **really understand** how business works when they make such infinitely naive comments about **profits and costs.**

If the regulator's fees and fines are not paid out of the payer's profits then they have to come out of capital, which would mean that capital reserves would diminish or the fines would have to be borrowed from the bank.

The **hefty fines** levied against life assures must surely take the biscuit. The regulator **'protects and gives comfort'** to the consumer by extracting a fine of say £700,000, FROM THE MUTUAL FUNDS OF THE COMPANY THAT ARE THE PROPERTY OF THE CONSUMERS THAT **THE REGULATOR** PURPORTS TO BE PROTECTING AND GIVING COMFORT TO.

With such a view on life does that place Caroline Instance, the head of OPRA, who made the offending comment, and *Mrs Bucket*, who takes her financial support from her own environment for granted, whilst bustling around looking important and **telling other people how to run their lives,** on anything but a parallel path.

The agricultural scene is not quite as idyllic as perhaps is painted in '*The Darling Buds of May*'. What a tremendous series that was and how archetypal of the image that many people have of the small farmer/market gardener. The **reality** is rather a **long way** from Ma and Pa Larkin.

Indeed, rather than neatly laid tables, experience shows rather stark wooden refectory facilities which are in the kitchen with maybe a cold ham sat on a wooden chopping board in the middle of it, surrounded by debris from previous gastronomic experiences, a butter and sugar dish and a bread board.

Life is **extremely basic** for the majority of smallholders and it gets more and more basic as **margins become thinner and thinner.**

The idyllic life of *Pa Larkin*, with his rotund and robust wife and bevy of children, only seeks to perpetuate the illusion that dealing in cash and tax avoidance make available the opportunity to lead the 'high life'.

The financial penalties for running private cars on tractor diesel are such that any farmer with any degree of sanity would not even contemplate the practice let alone engage in it. The myriads of inspectors, both veterinary and agricultural, provide a constant reminder to the farming fraternity that heavy fines are just around the corner if even the smallest part of the **regulatory regime** is transgressed.

There are *Pa Larkin* characters that flaunt the occasional Rolls-Royce; however, they also do more than their fair share of wedding engagements, the receipts for which go through the books, helping them to survive and **pay for the image**.

"BREACH OF PROMISE"

In 1998 farmers were signing contracts to grow peas for the frozen food industry to **receive payments of £90,000** when it was costing them **£100,000 to plant and harvest** the crop. Industrial coercion in the knowledge that a fleet of pea viners at several hundred thousand pounds each, purchased on finance, and used for a mere few weeks out of a 12-month period, for harvesting the peas, is an incentive for any **farmer to lose money just in the hope of staying alive for another season.**

It is a tragic example of the most distasteful side of what is laughingly called commercial enterprise. Many of the buyers and negotiators for the large

151

supermarkets and chain stores have codes of conduct akin to Al Capone rather than the Harvard Business School.

Where *Pa Larkin* would have bought his gas guzzling ex-army lorry for cash from a war surplus trader in 1946, **the modern day farmer** and agricultural haulier need to find substantial sums per month just to pay the hire purchase or lease on the vehicles they use, pay for their fuel as it goes into their storage tanks and **part with equally substantial fees** to the Government, before they ply their trade, **or be forced out of business.**

Analysis would show that **two-thirds of the workforce are employed** with the sole purpose of **providing income** to the **other third** that spend 100 **per cent of their time telling the first two-thirds how to run their lives.**

Consider the year 2000 agricultural and livestock prices.

Farm gate prices for milk have been reduced by 24 per cent over the four years to 1999. The British farmer gets paid 18.5p per litre for milk in the millennium year 2000, **the supermarket** take 99p per litre over the counter. **An uplift of more than five times**.

Slaughtered and processed beef is 94p per kilo. The **price** is multiplied by **five** to **twelve times in the supermarket** by the time it gets to the checkout.

Over the past 10 years shop prices have increased by 48 per cent.

Farm gate prices have increased by less than 2 per cent. There is something wrong with the mechanism: and it all comes back to the supermarkets. **The fanciful notion that consumers are getting the benefit of lower farm prices is a myth.** Many rural butchers produce their meat at a far lower cost over the counter than do the supermarkets.

THE RISK/REWARD RATIO

The truth is that **those who take all of the risks in production** are being coerced into subsidising those who feed off their hard work.

Arable prices are just as dire. Farmers are being forced to accept contract prices that are below production costs just to stay in business.

This is survival; not a commercial enterprise. In early 2000 the cost of producing a ton of potatoes was £77. The crop leaves the farm gate at between £50-£60 per ton and arrives on the supermarket shelf at £270 per ton.

The grower sustains a loss of 29 per cent or £12 for every ton of potatoes that leaves the farm. You cannot put them back in the ground to store for later! There is **NO SUBSIDY**. Just hope.

The farmer deserves, and should have, just reward for hard work done. You should ensure that he gets a fair return by selective purchasing from specialist outlets.

The grower may well deliver the crop to the supermarket. The situation is immoral. The seller makes a profit of more than 500 PER CENT, and uses it to **tighten the grip,** not only on the producers, but also on the Government **departments** implementing favourable regulation and legislation, not to mention planning advantages, that suit them.

Small retail greengrocers may well collect, clean, pack, and pay 'up front' for the produce they purvey, thus they **share the risk** to a far greater extent. The distribution network for potatoes has been cut back by central processing plants, which have bought out the competition and put **farmers in an untenable position.**

Wheat is one of the few commodities that make a profit at the farm gate of £20 per ton. Most of that is subsidy.

Farmers have never felt so **isolated** in terms of **public sympathy** and their physical situation. Few people work on farms any more. The work is all done by machinery to ensure that the crop is harvested at the right time.

People have been educated out of jobs that demand constant physical effort. They have become supermarket 'buyers' instead.

The economic pressures of the supermarket have swung too far for farmers to survive in the longer term. **But who, then, will own the land and produce the crops?**

Yes there are world prices: but who are they set by? A handful of international commodities' traders make the international markets between them and control prices to their own advantage.

Any market place needs balance, agriculture is no exception. Political interference is the primary cause of the current dilemma, the message outlining the remedy is not getting through.

Perhaps a novel remedy would be for the small town, or even village, traders to use the **'free bus' facility**. The 'free bus' service so thoughtfully arranged to take the customers from their local shops to the 'out-of-town' supermarket could provide the answer.

Buses have to go out to come back to travel to the rural market and shops, as well as taking people into their urban experience. The **rural traders** could therefore invite the 'townies', who have more net spendable income, to 'experience a **real shopping treat**, in real shops that give **service and choice'**.

By using the 'out-of-town' car park, conveniently located adjacent to the supermarket, they can travel on the free bus to the **beautiful rural environment** to shop at leisure and enjoy the local hostelry or tea-shop.

Whatever they **fail to find** that is better or cheaper than the supermarket they can **pick up on their return** to the car park where their car will be waiting, or the local bus will take them home.

VERMIN RIGHTS VERSUS COMPLIANT INNOCENCE

Fox hunting is another case in point.

Mr Blair (a surname which always reminds me of those little woolly animals which run around in fields and are harassed by foxes, particularly at their most vulnerable time, lambing) brings this topic into play every time he is in a corner. Even the **London mayoral election campaign** suddenly found the topic compelling. Perhaps the **Barbican Hunt** just has not come to full prominence yet?

However, I digress, **fox hunting** is, of course, a barbaric sport conducted by people who ride around the countryside on their own horses, on their own land, killing their own vermin in their own way. The hunting process is, of course, barbaric because it involves the mutilation of animals (foxes). They are caught by other animals (the hounds) whose sole purpose in life is to hunt down and kill foxes.

The foxes, apparently, die in an instant, torn to shreds by their assailants, much the same as any other predator, including a fox, might dispose of its prey.

EMOTIONAL SMOKESCREENING

Apparently **the discomfiture** of the majority of people, according to the press, is **that people should actually enjoy watching this spectacle**.

How many of the protagonists paid to watch 'JAWS' and 'JAWS II'?

How many enjoy the regular nature programmes in their living-rooms?

Of course, the fact of the matter is that by the time they, the spectators (huntsmen), arrive on the scene, the hounds have all but disposed of the fox.

There has to be, therefore, some other reason why fox hunting takes place.

The hounds are obviously there to dispose of the fox, which is a pest. The fox harasses lambs, chickens, ducks and anything else it can get its irrational teeth into. **The fox kills for pleasure**, not necessarily food. It will leave beheaded animals and badly mutilated carcasses of lambs just where they fall after it has had its pleasure chasing and killing them.

The **fox population** is managed by the 'countryside management team', largely farmers but also a lot of other people, including computer operators and people who just want to ride their horses in something other than the St Ledger or The Grand National.

Oh, that's the reason people go hunting, **to ride their horses** in the countryside, **at their leisure** without the extreme costs associated with 'steeple chasing' and 'horse racing', **without bookies taking bets** on who is going to get the fox (as in greyhound racing: although they chase a mock hare).

This exercise, apparently, not only benefits the human beings, who may well sit behind a desk or tractor steering wheel, or in a combine harvester cab for a large proportion of their day, but it also exercises the horses and prepares them for some of the very well supported public show jumping and racing events.

It is **a spontaneous sport.** It is not every time the hunt goes out that it actually finds something to chase. **Most foxes, seemingly, get away**.

MICE, RATS AND MOLES?

How do you dispose of mice, rats and moles?

Of course, a lot of people are lucky enough not to be plagued with them but when you have **80 in a roof space** of an old cottage, then poison is the answer.

One of the most efficient departments in a local council employs the 'rat- catcher'.

However, **the little nipper**, a wooden mouse-trap that snaps cleanly on the mouse's neck as he comes for the cheese, is a very efficient and economical way to deal with the odd mini-rodent.

What about rats? Well, a Jack Russell or a terrier is a good deterrent for rats but, of course, if **hunting with dogs** is not allowed and becomes a criminal act, how are farmers going to **clear their barns**?

Of course, if the act does become law then what one could do is **exclude vermin** or the hunting of vermin.

But there we are, back to the fox again. It strikes me that they will also have to find that nice **truffle** stuff that we have in chocolates in a different way. Truffle **hounds will be banned** as well, it seems.

It is an odd sort of society that **allows people** to set fire to cars, create malicious disorder and damage, deface buildings and publicly declare their **intent to cause mayhem**, but football supporters doing the same thing are jailed and banned from watching a match for three to five years.

It is difficult to know what the Equal Rights Commission would make of it but the Human Rights Commission seems to have got something **entirely wrong**.

The question to ask would be; are **more** animals **mistreated in the homes** of suburbia, abused, in pain, and under-fed, **than** are the number of **foxes** that are **traumatised**, according to the RSPCA newspaper advertisement, by fox hunting?

Perhaps the target of the abuse, arson and fanciful daubings would be better placed elsewhere. But then **bigotry would not be the same without a cause**, would it?

OUTLAW OR GUNLAW

An alternative to fox hunting on horseback, or even by the huntsman with his hounds on foot (and there is a spectacle to behold) is poison, a rather

157

slow and lingering death for the fox and his family. Or, of course, there is the much preferred option of shooting the fox. But doesn't shooting involve guns? **And are guns those lethal weapons that so many people are seeking to ban?**

Having **closed down** all of the small-bore **shooting galleries** which people enjoyed going to with their pistols to **actually improve** their ability to **hit a target**, there is now a move to ban those firearms in private possession. So who is going to kill the foxes?

You see, you cannot use a twelve-bore to kill a fox, you have to use a very accurate sighted rifle. Without such a weapon, the fox would have a good chance of being maimed and once again die a long lingering death in extreme pain.

Foxes cannot heal themselves. A dog, if it gets injured, can lick its wound and heal itself. A fox, apparently, cannot. A fox cannot lick a wound and clean itself up. It will **just die**. Quite interesting. So if the fox is shot and wounded then it will die anyway; but a long and lingering and **very painful death.**

And where would these marksmen come from? Who are going to fire such guns?

Well, as we would not have any of our own (having banned all of the small-bore ranges and the rifle range) are we perhaps to import them from **America** where they make all the films that **so many people watch in their homes,** perhaps even **encouraging their children** to watch them too, involving guns?

THE SPANISH OPTION

Or perhaps we could import marksmen from Spain, as we do our **'Inspectorate veterinaries'.**

158

They are cheap, do not speak good English, can do a good imitation of 'Manuel' from *'Fawlty Towers'* and if they miss the target, they will not understand the abusive language ranged against them. Perfect.

One of the **great paradoxes** of modern morality is that people **condemn** those who ride around on horses following the hounds, supposedly arriving at the scene, after two or three hours riding, of a fox being slowly dismembered by hounds apparently using 'knives and forks', they take so long to discharge their duty.

And yet **those same people who complain** watch documentaries with hippopotami being torn apart by lions, hyenas feasting on an antelope's bones, elephants being ripped apart by vultures, fish being gobbled up with great glee by predators, young albatrosses being devoured by sharks and so on. **Yet THAT is not ghoulish?** Indeed **blood-spattered television screens are the norm in our homes.**

When it is not animals gorging on each other (such an unnatural thing), it is people crashing through glass, spraying machine-gun bullets everywhere or using high-powered rifles to 'pick off' somebody in a car.

Somehow, gratuitous television gore and explicit violence is acceptable.

Of course, it has nothing to do with class, and 'them and us'. It has nothing to do with the chap at the factory gates watching the boss go through with his Rolls-Royce saying to his mate **'why can't he ride a bike like the rest of us'** as opposed to **'one day you know, Harry, I'm going to drive a car like that.'** It has nothing to do with that.

However, it has everything to do with the whole issue of people riding around on horses chasing a **defenceless fox**, which when it gets the chance, **will destroy every bird in a chicken-house** full of twenty, thirty hens and just leave them dismembered in pools of blood or, perhaps if it is hungry, take one home to his family to feast on.

The fact that the chickens may well represent **the livelihood** of a person owning a smallholding, living on a pittance, is soon lost on those with average earnings of £15,000 - £20,000 a year and a wide-screen TV. Many **farmers** struggle to eke out a living **to bring food to the table** of many of **their protagonists**. They have a right to manage their own environment.

If we, **as a society**, ban so called blood-lust in the field, surely we must **ban it in all places** of entertainment, including the home and cinema!

That moral issue is put to one side when it comes to entertainment, or even when slaughtering three million cattle because of the chance of BSE affecting 'humans'. Are we **so** important?

Society did not bother testing those animals; it just got rid of them.

But it is not that easy to do, is it? Three years after they were slaughtered the politicians were looking to store **six hundred thousand tons of minced dried carcasses awaiting disposal** on a disused airfield at Blyton in Lincolnshire.

Half the world is starving.

There is still no scientific link between BSE and CJD. CJD is arguably eminently preferable, yet less likely to happen, than starvation in most Third World countries.

Beef is a great source of protein, iron and calcium, which those particular people need, and **we condone slaughtering three million cattle** for no good reason other than they <u>may</u> suffer from a disease that only affects cattle anyway. **And members of parliament** and the media devote time and valuable resources **to ban fox hunting?**

Politics is about emotion.

Well, it is about time that 'society' **got emotional** about the livelihoods of those who **put food on their plates** day in and day out, and allow many in our society the luxury of two or three holidays a year; not bothering to dig their garden, not bothering to grow vegetables, not bothering to rear livestock, because **someone else does it for them.**

The farming group of people do not have index-linked earnings-related pensions to look forward to. Most will work well beyond the point where others have retired; **because they have to, to survive.**

We use the word 'amoral' when somebody has no morals, but I am lost for words when it comes to describing those who **have no understanding**, no empathy, with other sections of the community.

The Countryside March through London signified the depth of feeling concerning that lack of understanding of those who live in towns and cities (those who, perhaps, even feed foxes at their back door).

What you may not know is that professional 'catchers' catch 'town' foxes, which are now more prevalent than they have ever been, put them into lorries and just **dump them in the countryside** on the vain, and rather **stupid assumption**, that the foxes will just 'fall back' into their natural habitat and be happy and contented in the green pastures and small woods that surround them.

How **naive** can people get when dealing with **a territorial animal** that has been spoilt by an abundance of food in a town or city that they have brought him from; only to **waste away and die from starvation** or be forced to **attack farm animals** and destroy someone's livelihood, in this 'green and pleasant land', that takes such a lot of hard work and effort to gain an existence from, for the small- to medium-sized farmer.

A KNIGHT TO REMEMBER

An item, which the *Sunday Telegraph*, in January 1998, called 'surreal', was the total absence of surprise when **Dr. John Patterson**, Chairman of the Government Spongiform Encephalopathy Advisory Committee (SEAC), was **knighted.**

'Dr. John' was the man who set off the 1996 BSE, CJD scare which resulted in **billions of pounds being spent incinerating millions of healthy cattle,** and which has subsequently cost tax payers more than any other single Government project in history, apart from the Trident missile programme. Strangely, **it was not SEAC** that recommended that these **perfectly healthy animals should be destroyed**. Dr. Patterson's recommendation was merely **to debone** the meat before it was eaten.

Having **not** been **responsible** for the **slaughter** the now knighted Sir John **was responsible** for the report that brought in the diktat that it would be a **criminal offence to sell prime ribs of beef**, T-bone steaks, or anything else on the bone.

Bizarre.

A full and CONCLUSIVE study should be carried out before any mass slaughter is ever carried out again.

Full compensation should be paid to the business owners who suffered commercial loss: preferably by those who made such an ill-conceived and disastrous decision.

To compensate CJD sufferers' relatives **from public funds**, in isolation, is a travesty.

Any action should be against the individuals in the civil service, not taxpayers, and should rely upon genuine proof of a connection between BSE and CJD.

For the public to pay **is inequitable** against the backdrop of other potential claimants.

CHAPTER 17

TALKING TO A BRICK WALL

It was a wall. A simple wall. At 8.00pm on a warm evening in Scunthorpe, approximately eighty members of the Local Town Council were assembled in the **splendid council chamber** of the Civic Building on Oswald Road. The Deputy Mayor was in full regalia and the meeting was in full flow.

This august body had recently taken away the casting vote from the Mayor and through its Chief Executive it had implemented a dogmatic and totally irrational decision **to disenfranchise all local tradesmen, particularly the self-employed small businessmen, from tendering for local Government work** in the Scunthorpe area. A direct labour force employed by the Council would conduct all work.

The livelihoods of hundreds of small artisans, one-man businesses through to those employing twenty or thirty skilled craftsmen would be affected by the decision.

MAKING A POINT

On this eventful evening, a **large sheet of polythene** was placed in front of the huge plate-glass windows and very adequate double doorway into the main hall of the Civic Building. **A group of the 'threatened' artisans arrived with a flat truck, some ready-mixed mortar and a large quantity of 'breeze blocks'.**

By 9.00pm a significant crowd, including journalists and TV crews had arrived to view the spectacle of **a 'U' shaped wall**, some 25 feet long from end to end, flanked on one side by a Union Jack and on the other side by a flag-bearer with the *National Federation of Self-Employed* flag indicating to all observers the overwhelming displeasure that was felt with the actions of the local council politicians and their 'officers'.

The idea had all started with a typical and well-used comment. The debate had been going on for months and months with the Scunthorpe Borough Council regarding the use of direct labour as more efficient compared to local tradesmen. The tradesmen and women had relied on local Government work for a long period of years. Many firms were in serious difficulties financially, endeavouring to maintain their workforce and avoiding bankruptcy.

"It's like talking to a brick wall."

A phrase we often use, but one which sparked an immediate response from the 'Federation' for that area.

"If it's like talking to a brick wall, **let's build one**."

And they did.

ACTING IT OUT

The spokesman entered the building through a side entrance and going into the seemingly massive Council Chamber located off the main entrance lobby, he stopped the debate mid-flow:

"I felt that I should just announce, ladies and gentlemen, that in view of the fact that talking to this Council is like talking to a brick wall, we have built one. You have just been bricked in."

There was a palpable silence. A look of disbelief from the Deputy Mayor showed the **incomprehensible nature of the statement.**

At that point two ushers converged, lifted the spokesperson up by his elbows, **"ooh they were strong,"** and heaved him unceremoniously out of the double doors of the chamber, into the lobby.

He walked back in the dimly lit hallway, past the glass façade, and looked out onto the brick wall that his colleagues had built. The sea of faces and lights on the other side were only visible at the extreme periphery of the entrance, through the **large 'picture windows'**. And what a picture it made.

The bricklayers were still putting the finishing touches to the top of the wall, which had then reached a height of eight feet. It really was a tremendous sight, but perhaps it was all in vain. The councillors appeared to have ignored what had been said to them, but had they?

WITHIN THE LAW

The side entrance provided an exit to resume the position with the Union Jack; just in time for **a police sergeant** to come and address one of the individuals gallantly placing mortar on another breeze block before putting it into place atop the wall.

"Who is responsible for this?" came the sergeant's booming voice.

"He is," came the lightly-tinged accent with a **gesticulation** in the direction of the Union Jack from a **trowel-laden hand.**

"What's going on?" said the police sergeant.

The organisers ushered him away from the working area and down to the back of the car park. It was quieter there.

He was told that the group of tradesmen were making a protest, peacefully, and that they would clean up after themselves once they had **made their point**.

The policeman insisted that they had "made their point" and that they should dismantle the wall from in front of this public building. Caution was urged.

Members of the *National Federation of Self-Employed* were there building the wall because they were extremely upset. They should be allowed to make their protest. **Then they would 'clean up'.**

By this time it was about 9.20pm and where there had just been plain glass it was now a **montage of faces** at all levels, up and down the glass, and along

165

the exposed portion of the now bricked-up doors: **all looking out in total disbelief.**

The point had been made. The wall could be dismantled. First of all it had to be explained, through the wall, that the local tradesmen had built it to show **the lack of communication between the Council and the citizens.** Dogma had no place in this decision-making process, the **Council was elected by individual members of society** and those members of society had now built the wall. **They agreed to take it down if a dialogue could be struck up**.

THE MAYOR REINSTATED

It was the **start of the end of the 'direct labour only' scheme,** and within a few months the Scunthorpe works department had returned to some normality, the Mayor had been reinstated, with his casting vote, and the Chief Executive had disappeared, probably to Siberia.

The wall? The breeze blocks and mortar were put back on the flat truck, the polythene sheet was rolled up and the police sergeant **could not even pursue the group for dropping litter**. It was only one of a number of initiatives at that time, but it proved that sometimes politicians do not appreciate that **other people have brains, and feelings, until some form of explicit action convinces them.**

Perhaps a few more walls should be constructed in other strategic positions. Making a point can still be like talking to a brick wall on occasions. The recent 'fuel protest' may be the vanguard of a new age of 'communication psychology' that could have been avoided.

"When you work from a position of impossibility then probability becomes remote.

When you work from a position of probability then possibility becomes absolute."

A QUESTION OF HONESTY

It is right that we should have paid officials to look after our interests.

It is right that those officials should be remunerated to the point where they **do not become corrupt** by trying to enhance inadequate pay.

However, two-thirds of all of the compensation paid in respect of pensions mis-selling **will go back into local authority** and large ex-nationalised **pension funds**. What has happened with those particular funds in recent years?

Tom **was 52** when he was retired. He was treated, for pension purposes, **as if he was 65.**

For every five years early that an individual retires you need almost DOUBLE THE FUND to provide the same benefits.

The **hidden cash effect** on a pension fund **that you pay through your local and national taxes** is almost **SIX TIMES the amount required at his normal retirement date**.

EARLY RETIREMENT COSTS

At current annuity rates, Tom's pension, **without inflation-proofing**, would require a capital sum of £230,000 to be 'reserved'. To meet his **early retirement package the sum of £1.5 million**, or more, is necessary. Falling annuity rates increase the amount even more.

Adding in the inflation-proofing is beyond contemplation.

His pension is supposedly a 'funded' pension scheme because it is a local authority scheme, yet eight years ago, when he retired under a special redundancy agreement, he picked up a substantial tax-free cash sum, plus an earnings-related pension for life. **Who picks up any <u>fund shortfall</u>?**

Within **two weeks Tom was back doing the same job** that he had been doing prior to his redundancy. It had taken the local authority that long (two weeks) to realise that they just had not got the expertise available to replace Tom's skills. **How could he have been redundant**?

So, was Tom unique? No, there were thousands of Toms all over the country and not just engineers, as he was, but teachers, senior staff nurses, nursing sisters, administrators, police, fire, clerical and other 'council employees' many of whom are now back in employment doing the same job that they did before.

And **you are paying their current salary IN ADDITION to their pension**.

It is immoral in itself, but when one considers the **effective depletion** of the supposedly funded **'pension funds'** through incompetence, where is the missing money to be made up from?

'MIS-SELLING' - A GOVERNMENT TOP-UP

Perhaps the **three billion pounds** clawed back from private 'insured' personal pensions will help?

One **London local authority** is reported to be **£386 million in deficit**. If it were an insurance company it would be fined, to finish it off, and then closed down. **PUBLIC RIDICULE WOULD BE THE ORDER OF THE DAY.**

Equitable Life IS AN EXAMPLE.

The original object of the redundancy exercise was to **reduce** the local and central Government pensions **liability** for the future. The plan was surely to reduce senior employees and save their salaries. Then employ **'new' staff on less generous terms** with less costly pension provision.

The response of an Australian local council, when they were shown the details of the British plan for scaling down their senior employees, about sums it up. Details of the redundancy/severance packages were sent out to Australia, as they had been quite **impressed by the ease with which UK local authorities had scaled down** their senior employees without industrial action, complaint or major industrial tribunal responses.

The fax came back from Australia containing just two words:

"DREAM ON."

Apparently somebody, at the Australian end, had actually looked at the FACTS of what the financial consequences were in using the British strategy, before being lured into the same disastrous position.

A THIRTY-FIVE YEAR RUN-OFF

Tom retired thirteen years early and they paid him his pension as if he had completed those thirteen years based upon his current salary.

No early retirement adjustment was imposed. A full tax-free cash sum was payable, though not contributed to. He had been working for the authority since he was twenty-six. Twenty-six eightieths entitlement became thirty-nine eightieths in payment. The maximum entitlement was forty eightieths so he was **only one year short** of a **full 50% pension. That is** indexed **for the rest of his life.**

In addition to that he had thirty-nine times three divided by eighty; times his salary as a senior engineer, **paid as a tax-free cash sum**, plus he had **£30,000 as a redundancy** payment, also tax-free. **The authority**, for sure, did not **wonder** why he was persuaded to leave.

He went back on a 'consultancy' basis and earned almost as much as he did for a five-day week, in three days, **self-employed!** The full enhanced pension is still paid by the same local authority.

The damage is done and those who got it wrong will not only escape paying for those mistakes, they will be **drawing earnings-related pensions** from the same source. And now there is the spectre of ex-military pensioners wanting to review the inflation 'rights' that were altered in the late 1970s because of the strain on the economy. Surely the line has to be drawn somewhere?

Clare was a teacher. The kids at school were driving her mad. Respect and authority had become things of the past and she was offered redundancy, **a five-year enhancement** to her pension plus **a contract to come back and do three days** because the school knew that they could not find another teacher to replace her. Even if she hadn't returned she could earn as much on three days "supply teaching" as she could on a full salary (but no paid holidays).

Steel workers, mine workers, employees right across the Governmental 'patch' evidenced people being paid **pensions out of the public purse** and then being **re-employed** in virtually the same job and **getting a salary** out of the public purse **a second time**.

Of course, some were not so lucky, they only had their enhanced pension.

There are those, lower down the pecking order, who lost out altogether. Private industries reliant upon Government contracts. **They just quietly disappeared,** along with their employees **to the Job Centres**.

There is an inequity in the way that our society works and it appears to be **those who create the rules** that are responsible.

Government has only public money to carry out its functions. It surely has **a duty of care** for the way it conducts itself. So consumed are we, the public, WITH SIDE SHOWS, like BSE and pensions mis-selling and endowments, that the REAL ISSUES like where our **tax money is squandered**, are lost.

CHAPTER 18

THE PROPAGANDA WAR

Cast your minds back to the Balkans War and ask yourself how many times you saw headlines that said "NATO Allies Destroy Four Tanks", or "Six Personnel Carriers Destroyed in Course of Attacking Village", or "NATO Brings Down Yugoslav Aircraft".

What were the headlines that you saw?

"Forty killed in a bus on a bridge."

"Fifteen civilians killed in hospital horror."

"Three killed in Chinese embassy."

"One hundred civilians killed in Kosovo village."

That is the power of **propaganda.**

WHAT IS NEWS?

In her naivety a journalist who had been three weeks out of University told me:

"93 per cent of all news is 'good news'. It's normal. We can't report what is normal. What we need to do is report what is **abnormal** and that is the bad news. **7 per cent** of everything that is happening is **bad news** and that's what we report."

It's what they feel they have got to report. **It's what 'they' call "news".**

At one time, at the beginning of the regulator's campaign to bring insurance companies 'into check' **a £60,000 fine was news**. Then the media really did not think that £60,000 was worth reporting so it became £100,000. It ended up in 1998 with a £900,000 fine. Why? Well, **the fine** fell into the 7 per cent bracket, which was news.

But what are the facts behind the news?

SELECTIVE REPORTING

Thousands upon thousands of **successful sorties flown**, Serb military positions destroyed or disadvantaged, but that falls to page eight or nine, which is the middle of the paper. It **is commentary**, normal news. If you want to read the detail you look in the commentary. The headlines always concentrated on the minority happenings and sensationalism.

Similarly, in the **pensions industry**, when the pensions mis-selling accusations first broke in the *Financial Times*, members of the Life Insurance Industry were asked the questions:

1   How many times have you sat **face-to-face with a new client**, in the last twelve months, and gone through a financial planning process **completing a fact find** to give advice?

2   How many of those people on **a one-to-one**, face-to-face basis, have <u>ever, since they took out their first policy,</u> **had** what you would call **bad advice?**

Then they were asked to do one more thing, **divide the latter number by the former**. Now some of them had difficulty with that, but they wrote the two figures plus their answer down on a bit of paper and the bits of paper were collected in. They were taken back to an **independent scrutineer**, who then worked through the numbers.

The investigation covered some **500 advisors** in five different locations spread around the country, and approximated to some **8000 clients** or potential customers. It was a reasonable sample when you **compare it** to

172

those used by the **Consumers' Association** and the **Office of Fair Trading** and similar bodies (a **sample of 30** out of **230,000**).

The highest percentage from one group was **6.3 per cent.** The average across 500-plus advisers was 5.6 per cent **had <u>ever</u> come into contact with bad advice**.

People in the industry are the biggest **whistle-blowers** that there are. If there is something wrong; if **somebody is 'stepping out of line'** these are the people who **'pull the plug'** on them. Anything, anything to take unfair competition or a disreputable figure out of circulation. The average was **5.6 per cent EVER**.

The headlines have **concentrated on** that **SMALL PERCENTAGE. Is that what this is all about?** 5.6 per cent of the insurance-buying public, OVER THEIR LIFETIME, have **received bad advice**?

ASKING THE WRONG PEOPLE

Interestingly enough, when the **survey was first carried out** some of the respondees, maybe three or **four or five** out of an audience of one hundred, were **coming up with 50 per cent and 60 per cent** had received bad advice. About half of those allowed themselves to be questioned afterwards about their answers. Several interesting facts emerged:

They were **not 'one-to-one' salespeople**.

Yes, they had had face-to-face interviews but they were not 'one-to-one' salespeople. These were **branch managers**. Those were the people who got the **problem policyholders** to look after.

If you were a politician who wanted to talk about mis-selling in the industry, **who would you go to, the salespeople or the managers?**

The managers. They have the overview, right? **WRONG!**

173

What is the manager's perception of mis-selling from his standpoint? - Surely it has to be **"over half the people I have seen have been mis-sold."**

The interesting fact is that they **only saw eight to ten people per year.** Eight to ten people per year and fifty – sixty per cent of those people had had a bad deal at some time in their life, which meant that **four or five people had been disadvantaged.** 'Four or five' out of hundreds of satisfied policyholders?

Is this really what the politicians are getting so upset about? The gentleman in charge of the Treasury investigation into mis-selling was asked why, **if he thought** that there was **a lack of confidence** by the public in the insurance industry, the public were **still buying ten million new policies** a year. He had no answer; save reference to the 'pensions mis-selling' scandal.

We only have a population of 58 million. Two-thirds of them are ineligible for virtually anything that would be appropriate to that 10 million statistic. That means just under **one-third of the population** are **buying new products** during any year. And **there is a lack of confidence?** Where is the evidence?

What would the market look like if **these people were confident** in what they were buying?

Of course, it could be that they are **buying the twelve-fourteen per cent compound annualised return** on **endowment policies** over a 25-year period.

It could be that they are **buying the fourteen - eighteen per cent compound annualised return** that has been achieved on twenty **year pension policies** in the past.

It could be that they are **buying into stock market returns of ten – twelve per cent per annum** compound as against building society and bank deposit account rates of 6 per cent. Could that be where the **confidence** is?

Maybe they just had not been reading the newspapers or maybe they were **just fools**.

TEN MILLION MISGUIDED FOOLS?

How many of you can recall the **intricate details** of an hour-long conversation with another individual on **technical matters** at the end of the meeting? **Without taking a note?** Well, that was what was expected by the **Consumers' Association** from their **researchers**.

The researcher for financial services **'mystery shopper'** was invariably **an actor**. Hired to learn certain lines to "become" a certain individual and enact the part in front of a financial adviser. The objective was to **establish the response** of that adviser to the circumstances of the actor and to scrutinise the advice that would be given, and report upon it.

Very seldom was there a second interview and, of course, the storyline would be basically the same with each adviser visited. **Transactions were never carried through** to completion. **Interviews lasted one to two hours.**

What the actor had to do **after the interview** was to retreat somewhere and **fill in a questionnaire** in some detail.

Many questionnaires read, "**very pleasant individual, got along well**" or words to that effect. **The magazine articles were uniformly damning**. Copies of those questionnaires were eventually made available, after the event, and therefore, we knew precisely what each contained.

After completion by the actor the questionnaires would be sent to one of the research organisation's **"accepted advisers"**.

That "accepted adviser" would **review the responses** on the questionnaire, **without reference to the actor (interviewer)**, to determine whether or not the advice given was "good", "bad" or "indifferent", and seemingly send comments back to the Consumers' Association, who would then forward them to the editor of Which? magazine.

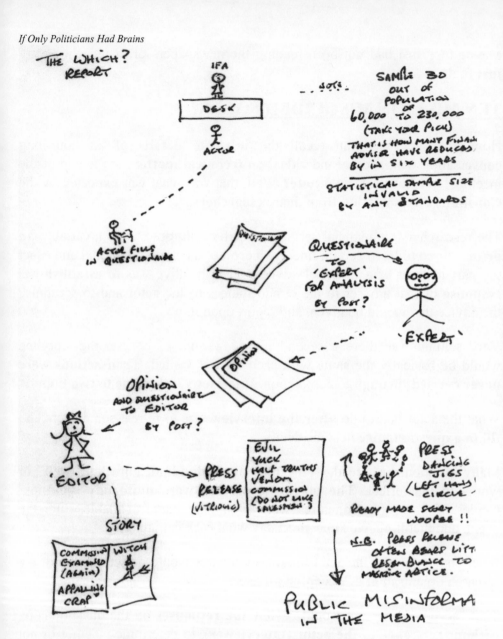

A 'journalist' would then, apparently, **write up 'the report'**.

Do you detect a likely **communication problem** in this system?

IMPLIED EXPERTISE

Each individual in the chain, including the financial adviser 'interviewer' who started it, and the PR person who finished it off, effectively **operated in a vacuum.**

This research was supposed to indicate to the public **how 'badly done to they were'** by expressions which are still used by the organisation regularly, **"ripped off", "appalling".**

It's become part of **the '*Which?* Dictionary'** standard. Now Gordon Brown, the Chancellor of the Exchequer has adopted the same tone with his **"Rip-off Britain".** Is there some connection?

Interestingly enough, the Woolwich Building Society became one of the "victims" of vitriol. They were accused of being **"commission hungry"** and "biased" when they advised the actor (cum 'would-be' client) to take out a three-year bond.

This was interpreted by the remote adviser to mean **an insurance bond** but, in actual fact, it was a deposit bond within the Building Society. The **cash deposit** had no insurance links whatsoever.

Very often people are **blinded by preconceived ideas**. The Woolwich were publicly hauled over the coals for biased "commission-hungry" advice. The product advised **did not incorporate commission.**

Bigotry at its best.

The real problem lies in the obsession with costs and the lack of understanding of the technical nature of the products. The same or similar terms are used for dissimilar products. The **historic returns of the 'commission' paying insurance bond** that was so vociferously condemned by *Which ? Magazine* have been around **10 per cent per annum compound**; almost **double what the non-commission bearing cash deposit 'bond'** produced.

THE 'BAD PUBLICITY' CARD

Unfortunately the life insurance and pensions industry 'backed off' taking 'a real swing' at the **unnecessary humiliation of individuals** caught up in this **clandestine exercise**, and has probably suffered as a result of that inactivity in the ensuing years.

There is only one way to 'mystery shop'. That is to have total commitment. **"Buy"** the product or service, analyse it and then **comment on the facts.**

In the aeronautical engineering field one did not just take any old bolt and put it into an aeroplane and hope that the wings didn't fall off. **It was felt that that was unfair to the passengers and the crew.** The engineers would **test** the metal **first**. Usually **to destruction**.

Whole aeroplanes, cars, trains and so on, are put through tests that seek to ensure the integrity of the finished product when it is sold to the public.

So it is with 'mystery shopping'. One has to go through 'the mill' and **complete the tests** to be of any value whatsoever. Only then can a **valued judgement** be made.

.

CHAPTER, 19

WHAT DOES ONE DO?

Life is so complex and the **flow of information so free and fulsome** that perhaps politicians can be excused for thinking that they are the only people who have brains, and regulators, for feeling that they are the only individuals with any experience (worth having that is).

The truth of the matter is that **those who engage in a profession, industry or trade** not only have brains and experience but they know how to use both to the good of those whom they serve so **much more effectively** on many occasions, than those who seek to govern and those who seek to dictate by regulation, their mode of operation.

Of course, there are countless other stories that could have been related within the pages of this brief, but hopefully **informative, review**.

One would not wish to become as expansive and verbose as those against whom we make our observations.

The **proliferation of words**; followed by words that explain what the original words meant, followed by a further publication of words issued to explain how one should interpret the first two books of words is not really the way we wish to live in a civilised society. Is **the rulebook** really the answer to the ills that perceptively, at least, pervade the fabric of our commerce and the private places of our personal conduct?

"Human justice will never right all the wrongs in the world."
Jesus of Nazareth

MORE GOOD THAN BAD

The **enlightened** will know that the majority of people in any population, civilised or not, are good, social, law-abiding, moral people who keep to the

code of their community, if not their country and their belief system, their God.

The most agnostic of **individuals exhibit all the traits of a moral code** that seems to be imbued within the majority of 'classes' of the human species. Indeed, if we go beyond our own form and look at **other animals** we find exactly the **same traits**.

Strangely, other animals can live **without written rules** and control freaks that wish to impose them. There seems to be a mechanism by which a natural order or hierarchy is achieved. The **strong** invariably lead and **nurture the weak**.

Should we, therefore, go back to mud huts or caves, clubs and spears and the odd loin-cloth? There are those who would argue we would do better with that system than we currently do with the one we have; they are **probably misguided**.

WHAT MAKES YOU THINK THAT?

There are basically ten rules that govern society, and if they were implemented by teaching them to our children and turning those children into responsible adults then, by and large, we would have little to fear.

Everyone should ask the question: "what makes you think that?" more often when a statement is made.

However, we are not governed by Government. Those who sit 'behind' Government govern us. They, in turn, appear to direct or **influence the media**. Our attention should be **focused upon them**.

And so we return to **the root** of our so-called civilised practice, those who seek to control use the media to propound their views and create mischief. The BSE crisis was borne of a tabloid newspaper's vitriolic attack on a Member of Parliament **for political gain**. The **cost** to the nation has been in the **billions of pounds** and is not over yet.

The reason we have so many **cars on the road** during term-time, conspicuously absent when 'school is out', is due to **the media** and the ghoulish indulgence of the public in every gory detail of every disruptive, indecent, illicit or sexual act against a member of the public, yet our society is probably **safer than it has ever been.**

Thanks to the media we are now 'scared' of going to the doctor, allowing our children to walk to school, or cycle, or catch the bus, or catch mumps, or measles, or be vaccinated against them. Many children are restrained from kissing their grandfather or grandmother or accepting a hug.

We are becoming a **denatured society** and the 'unnatural acts' that we perform are **the lack of physical contact with those we love.** Expressions of sympathy, compassion or simple friendship are avoided for fear that it **might turn against us** because of what we read or watch on our televisions.

The glass is permanently half empty. **The glass should be half full.**

We do not listen to grandma any more. The 'old wives' tales' often exhibit an insight into understanding 'modern' diseases and the simple solutions to them.

Children are advised against **a salt gargle**; but a **prescription medicine** to gargle with, certainly. Such is the **force of advertising.** Back to the media again.

Commerce is not bad; but the misdirection of commercial interest certainly is.

Like the brick wall in Scunthorpe, there is a time when a stand has to be made: and there is no time like the present.

HOW 'PC' CAN NAMES BE?

Why do we call medicines 'drugs'? We are surely trying to get children to take one; and **avoid** the other. Glaxo and Welcome are well-respected companies that produce **DRUGS.**

The saga of the wood and chopping board **highlights just how easily led** some of those in **authority can be** by those who wish to capitalise on their own 'preceptive' interests.

Pulling it all together, it seems that the chains of freedom are sometimes harsher than the chains of oppression.

We live in a free society that **imposes fines on its citizens for trivial rule breaches** and yet allows society's **delinquents to have special treatment** and individual attention.

Society condones and even **promotes promiscuity** and yet **preaches** about finding ways to **stop teenage pregnancies** and **control AIDS**.

We have **a media obsessed with sex and violence,** with inhospitable, antisocial behaviour the accepted 'norm'. Bad manners and a total disregard for authority are portrayed daily for our youngsters to mimic, cultivate and use against delegated authority.

What sort of adults and parents are we to allow such a travesty, and even promote such goings on?

The most basic societies, still living **in the depths of a jungle** somewhere, appear to have **far more respect for family, seniority, experience and morality** than we do, with our politicians who cannot even write their own speeches.

Some **denigrate nursery rhymes** and **applaud 'SPIN'**. Both are fiction, society has to decide which is the more harmful in our cultural development.

TAKING RESPONSIBILITY

The final shocker comes from the construction industry where a major company was asked to fit windows of a certain specification, but the 'spec' was not available. **The client then put forward an alternative** which the builders felt was inferior, and voiced their opinion regarding the potential lack of performance.

The client insisted that the alternative specification was okay.

Three years later an industrial tribunal found **against the builders for installing the windows,** because a female worker had lost her hand as a result of the reflective glare from the windows that had been fitted. The builders were told by the tribunal chairman that **they should not have fitted the particular product**, even though their **client** (who had brought the action against them) **had signed specific authority** for the fitters **to do so.**

Our society must learn to take **responsibility for its own actions** and turn **away from** this consumer culture of **'who can we blame'** and **'where can we get compensation from.'**

THE VESUVIUS ANSWER

The conversation on the train centred very firmly on the **overreaction** to the problems that **Railtrack** had had with a broken rail at the scene of the Hatfield railway accident. The mind is easily concentrated on such esoteric topics when **travelling at fifteen miles an hour** in a high-speed train on a straight track.

The lawyer was of Italian extraction: her **father was Sicilian**. They come from a village just outside of Naples, which, of course, sits in the shadow of **Mount Vesuvius, a volcano**.

The **speciality** area of law for the lady's practice was **environmental law,** the conversation mused upon whether the **Parish Council of her Sicilian village** would be **culpable** if Vesuvius erupted, because 'they should have gone round and told people that it **might erupt.**'

Taking the journey that the threesome were 'enjoying', and the regulatory experiences of the individuals in **their own professional environments**, they decided that if the mountain was in the **United Kingdom** the Parish Council should actually **pay the residents compensation in expectation of Vesuvius erupting.**

Alternatively, the **builders** of the houses would be **ordered to pay** compensation for **enticing the residents** to live in such a **dangerous place.**

Daft, isn't it?. But that is basically what is happening in our society. Those in authority **are trying to foresee far too much.** As human beings we are **all fallible.**

WITH 'RIGHTS' GOES RESPONSIBILITY

Statutory regulation must be curtailed, as must the inexorable growth of bureaucracy and its harbingers of impending doom. Self-regulation is far more efficient and discerning than the state-sponsored bodies. The law is a remedy for transgressors.

Relevant and authentic research must be a precursor to Government intervention and action.

Government officials must be accountable. Where appropriate they should be personally responsible for their errors, if they are negligent.

The public deserve better than the **instant fix, reactionary** form of Government that is currently in evidence. Children would be admonished for acting with such **inappropriate and wasteful haste.**

The **'free press' is too free** for the good of society.

The Press Complaints Commission requires a full and effective overhaul to ensure impartiality and objectivity. Prejudgements concerning accidents, criminal acts and matters of public health should be subject to compensatory scrutiny. A body which ignores its own guidelines clearly **fails to meet the standards expected of it by the public.**

184

Surely it is **wrong to pre-empt** a court judgement or a **board of enquiry**?

Millions of lives have been thrown into turmoil by headline-seeking editors closely associated with **publicity orientated 'experts'**. The public deserves better.

"The greater the level of regulation and prescription the greater the number of informal economy workers and society-created criminals."

Chinese saying

COMMON SENSE AND THE TEN COMMANDMENTS ARE ALL THE GUIDANCE WE NEED

Politicians should **get out more**. There is little doubt that a number of politicians lack empathy with **their constituents**.

Academics and bureaucrats hold the front line of the politician's thought process whilst both ignore the practicalities of carrying through government diktats.

Politicians should visit the work places they condemn, talk to those whom they purport to represent, **arrive unannounced**. I shall never forget Margaret Beckett, MP for Lincoln some years ago, stating that she would do what she thought was right for her constituents; **no matter what the constituents said.**

The **attitude** also reflects the more up-to-date **condemnation** of endowments linked to **mortgages** by Paul Flynn MP from Cardiff who, when asked for his **authority** in making the statement that they were made value for money, referred to **articles** in the *Financial Mail* and the *Sunday Times*. **Where is the research?**

Every with-profit e**ndowment, securing a mortgage** that has matured, has paid the mortgage and left the policyholder with a **significant surplus. Every one.**

Whilst the public would **not benefit** from the return of the old **'D' notice** which prohibited the press from making comment on sensitive issues, it is surely not in the public interest to go through the absurd and, in many ways, **frightening machinations** of press generated scaremongering that we have experienced over the last twenty years.   And it gets worse.

Controls are never adequate but redress has to be.

The press are very **quick** to point out **others' inadequacies** but always run to 'freedom of the press' to **hide their own**.

Jeff Prestridge at the *Financial Mail on Sunday* and Tony Hazell on the *Money Mail*, a mid-week equivalent, along with their other financial journalist colleagues, have a **huge responsibility** to those whom they seek to deliver **financial guidance** to.

Journalists must surely be answerable for giving **opinion that is incorrect** and guidance that is based upon a **false premise**.

Often, senior writers such as Liz Dolan from the *Sunday Telegraph* and the writing of would-be responsible financial journalists like Diana Wright (*Sunday Times*) are over-shadowed by **irresponsible rantings** from those who, for some obscure reason, become financial journalist of the year.

Few, if any, **have qualifications** or indeed long-term market experience in the arenas that they seek to condemn.

For all her other outstanding features, Charlie Dimmock would surely not be able to carry off her work as a TV presenter on gardening, and particularly water-feature matters, could she not **display adequate talents** in the **subject matter**.

Those who **pronounce publicly** on matters of importance should be **qualified** before being allowed to do so, not just **academically** but **experientially** also.   There may be a right to freedom of the press, but with that right goes **responsibility,** and with that responsibility the public are entitled to a level of **competence** that is **sadly lacking** at present.

All those journalists who have been named **have been reported** to the Press Complaints Commission and all their **mis-statements upheld** as **opinion,** and anyone, it seems, is entitled to publish their opinion.

Having **received confirmation** of that fact no less than three times from the **Press Complaints Commission,** they give me **full justification for printing mine.**

That still, however, does not make the present press modus operandi right. **'Can one blind man guide another?'** **Surely both will fall into a pit.**

'...why do you observe the splinter in your brother's eye and never notice the plank in your own?' *Luke's Gospel*

The hypocrisy of politicians, civil servants and the media, who are all **privileged to be in a position of influence** over society, is in their own inability to accept that **humanity is fallible.**

THE ANSWER TO THE PROBLEM

Politicians should visit hospitals, schools, production and service centres unannounced and unfettered to see how they really work day by day.

Regulators should be in touch with the real world rather than the Walter Mitty world of current practice.

Those with financial and political clout will **throw up smokescreens,** as has been seen, playing to the crowd and deluding those who may well have a genuine urge to redress social wrongs and impart a form of justice.

The promiscuity of the sixties and seventies is now reverberating through society at all levels.

Whilst one can promote **safer sex**, safe sex is a Utopian dream that can never be fulfilled. **The only 'safe sex' is 'no sex'.**

Our youngsters **deserve a better example** from those who seek to guide them as responsible adults. Surely in a society that relies very heavily upon television as a means of entertainment and communication, the **demarcation line** for bad language and so-called **adult practice** should be nearer to **11.00pm** than the current 9.00pm 'watershed'.

If we accept that changes in society allow bad language and promiscuous sex, then we must also acknowledge that teenagers of **fourteen and fifteen** years of age are certain to be viewers of television and listeners to radio **well after 9.00pm**.

Even the night club experience does not usually start in earnest until after the pubs have closed at 10.30 or 11.00pm. Let **those who want** that sort of entertainment experience it **after the majority** have experienced high-quality entertainment. The remedy is in your hands.

It only takes **ten letters of complaint** to have any programme on television or radio completely reviewed.

Politicians have to understand that **incoherent letters** are borne of anger not illiteracy. Frustration creates verbal inconsistencies which **politicians have a responsibility** to cut through and **analyse**.

Members of Parliament's complaints about a high workload **reflect badly** on their understanding of just how much it takes to rear animals on a farm, manufacture the items in everyday life that the public take for granted and provide **the services** that complete the infrastructure of our **complex society.**

There are no right and wrong answers, only levels of understanding, acceptance and assistance.

Giving service is not dictating terms. It is on that understanding that politicians will realise that **we all have brains** and even in our limited

188

capacity to use them on occasions, we should be **treated with respect** and **have those views listened to**.

Other books by the same author:

Mountains out of Molehills

Motor Cycles and Side-Cars
Mountains Out of Molehills uses the
familiar to explain the unfamiliar,
humorous to explain the technical,
common-sense and plain-speaking throughout

A starter manual on life assurance,

Invaluable for trainee sales staff of Life Assurance companies or for
individuals who are interested in looking after their affairs and
wondering about obtaining their own life assurance.
**The perfect companion for those studying for their Financial
Planning Certificate**.
Buy *Whole Life* instead of *Term*. Know how *Unit Linked* and *With
Profit* works.

"This is where selling to family and Business all starts

You Sign

'Trusts' A Practical Guide

TRUSTS - A Practical Guide is intended as a practical understanding of
the use of trusts in financial planning.

"A Terrific Book"   Keith Popplewell (Trainer and Speaker)

"'TRUSTS' Got me through my trust exams."

Barry (Sheffield Region Committee

*"Brilliant: absolutely brilliant - I now understand a lot more about hov
trusts work"*   John Watson Middlesborough Dec 99

Great returns. The *'COSTS'* myth exploded. With Profits Better? This
book examines the figures. It points to the definitive long term saving
structure. The best of all worlds.

*"Full of useful 'Point of Discussion' facts that show just how good the
Insurance industry returns actually are . Excellent."*
Brendan Burns FSB Policy Committee Chairman

'Stakeholder Pensions' A Practical Guide

FEES? - IT IS TIME TO GET REAL – INVEST FOR YOURSELF – GET 'FEE-PAC'™

Stops time wasters	Ensures payment for your Professional time
Lets your clients have a choice	Is something that you can develop with ease
Helps you spend your time better	Eliminates complicated jargon and systems
Has an easy to follow format and	Includes full "Start to Finish" documentation
Uses commission income efficiently	Does not require hours of training, complicated techniques or computer

The full cost is only £300 (inc VAT). (You are giving that much away with every **FREE CONSULTATION**

Book Order Form

Book Title	Book Cost	Post & Packing	Cost Inc P & P	No of Copies	Total Cost
If Only Politicians Had Brains ™	£14.95	£3.05	£18.00		
Other books by the same author					
Mountains out of Molehills™	£20.00	£3.00	£23.00		
You sign™	£9.95	£1.55	£11.50		
'Trusts' – A Practical Guide™	£25.00	£3.00	£28.00		
'Stakeholder Pensions' – A Practical Guide™	£25.00	£3.00	£28.00		
Parents' Poetry (Judy Theobald)	£4.50	£0.50	£5.00		

Name:

Address:

Postcode:

Date: Order Ref:

Single Payment Bankers Order

To: Bank

Address:

Postcode:

Please pay the sum of £ .... (in words:) to:

Life Publications Ltd, The Royal Bank of Scotland,
13 Stonebow Centre, LINCOLN LN2 5DL

Account No: 12515560
Sort Code: 16-23-32

Name of account:

Account No.:

Sort Code:

Signed   Date:

Book Order Form

Book Title	Book Cost	Post & Packing	Cost Inc P & P	No of Copies	Total Cost
If Only Politicians Had Brains ™	£14.95	£3.05	£18.00		
Other books by the same author					
Mountains out of Molehills™	£20.00	£3.00	£23.00		
You sign™	£9.95	£1.55	£11.50		
'Trusts' – A Practical Guide™	£25.00	£3.00	£28.00		
'Stakeholder Pensions' – A Practical Guide™	£25.00	£3.00	£28.00		
Parents' Poetry (Judy Theobald)	£4.50	£0.50	£5.00		

Name: _____

Address: _____

_____

Postcode: _____

Date: _____   Order Ref: _____

Single Payment Bankers Order

To: _____ Bank

Address: _____

Postcode: _____

Please pay the sum of £ ……….. (in words:) to:

Life Publications Ltd, The Royal Bank of Scotland,
13 Stonebow Centre, LINCOLN LN2 5DL

Account No: 12515560
Sort Code: 16-23-32

Name of account: _____

Account No.:

Sort Code:

Signed _____   Date: _____

Book Order Form

Book Title	Book Cost	Post & Packing	Cost Inc P & P	No of Copies	Total Cost
If Only Politicians Had Brains ™	£14.95	£3.05	£18.00		
Other books by the same author					
Mountains out of Molehills™	£20.00	£3.00	£23.00		
You sign™	£9.95	£1.55	£11.50		
'Trusts' – A Practical Guide™	£25.00	£3.00	£28.00		
'Stakeholder Pensions' – A Practical Guide™	£25.00	£3.00	£28.00		
Parents' Poetry (Judy Theobald)	£4.50	£0.50	£5.00		

Name: _____

Address: _____

_____

Postcode: _____

Date: _____ Order Ref: _____

Single Payment Bankers Order

To: _____ Bank

Address: _____

Postcode: _____

Please pay the sum of £ ……….. (in words: _____) to:

Life Publications Ltd, The Royal Bank of Scotland,
13 Stonebow Centre, LINCOLN LN2 5DL

Account No: 12515560
Sort Code: 16-23-32

Name of account: _____

Account No.:

Sort Code:

Signed _____ Date: _____

35788112R10204

Printed in Great Britain
by Amazon